Mom:

- Do you want the best for your son?
- Do you hope that he'll succeed in life?
- Do you wish you understood boys better? (After all, you didn't have any brothers, or if you did, you sure didn't understand them either.)
- Are there times your son thinks so differently from you that you're not quite sure how to relate or respond?
- Does his "maleness" sometimes disturb, annoy, or disgust you?
- Do you long for him to have strong, healthy friendships and a good relationship with you when he leaves home?
- Do you hope to have a great daughter-in-law someday who can also be a friend?
- Do you hope your son will be a good daddy?

If these are your dreams and wishes for yourself and your son, *What a Difference a Mom Makes* is the book for you. I guarantee it.

What a
Difference a
mom
Makes

What a Difference a mom Makes

*The Indelible Imprint a Mom
Leaves on Her Son's Life*

Dr. Kevin Leman

Revell

a division of Baker Publishing Group
Grand Rapids, Michigan

© 2012 by Kevin Leman

Published by Revell
a division of Baker Publishing Group
P.O. Box 6287, Grand Rapids, MI 49516-6287
www.revellbooks.com

Printed in the United States of America

Library of Congress Cataloging-in-Publication Data
Leman, Kevin.
    What a difference a mom makes : the indelible imprint a mom leaves on her son's life / Dr. Kevin Leman.
        p. cm.
    Includes bibliographical references.
    ISBN 978-0-8007-2173-2 (cloth)
    ISBN 978-0-8007-2211-1 (international trade paper)
    1. Mothers and sons—Religious aspects—Christianity. I. Title.
BV4529.18.L46 2012
306.874'3—dc23   2012009168

To protect the privacy of those who have shared their stories with the author, some details and names have been changed.

The internet addresses, email addresses, and phone numbers in this book are accurate at the time of publication. They are provided as a resource. Baker Publishing Group does not endorse them or vouch for their content or permanence.

12   13   14   15   16   17   18   7   6   5   4   3   2   1

To my wonderful son,
Kevin Anderson Leman II

I'd love to take credit for the
great man you've turned out to be,
but this book points out the obvious:
Mom had a great deal more to do with it than I did.
You've won six Emmys, you're the head writer
and an executive producer of the
funniest daytime TV program,
but what makes me proudest is the
respect and care you show to others,
your humble nature, your faith in God,
and your love for your family.

Contents

9

Acknowledgments

To my mother, May Leman, because I know firsthand what a difference moms can make in their son's life.

To my dear wife, Mrs. Uppington, because I've seen the difference she's made in our son's life—and so has the world.

To my editor, Ramona Cramer Tucker, who gets what boys of all ages—including myself and her adventurous, fun-loving, go-for-the-goal husband, Jeff—are about.

To my stellar Revell team, including Lonnie Hull DuPont, editor extraordinaire, and Jessica English, who fine-tunes my manuscripts to their brightest sheen.

Introduction

Boys Will Be Boys—Always

You panic. "I don't know a thing about boys!"
Ah, but you will.

You've always dreamed of having that precious little daughter—one who is a little replica of you. You dream of the close relationship you'll have as mother and daughter, watching her taking her first step, buying her first tutu for her ballet recital, arranging her hair for her first date . . .

And then you show up at the doctor's office for your sonogram.

"What's that?" you say, pointing at a little something you can't quite place on the blurry black-and-white image.

And the doc says, "That's a penis."

You frown, not understanding. "My daughter's got a penis?" Then realization dawns. "A boy?"

Inside you start to panic. *What do I do with a boy? I don't know a thing about boys!*

Ah, but you will.

Maybe you weren't raised with any siblings, or at least with any brothers. Perhaps your dad was MIA, so you didn't get much guy influence in your house. Or maybe you did have a brother, but you didn't understand him then . . . or now.

"My daughter's got a penis?"

Or perhaps you're already thrown into the process of bringing up your boy. He might be an infant you recently birthed or adopted, and you're congratulating yourself because you just figured out how to strategically place the Pampers so you don't get those early-morning or late-night surprise showers when you change his diaper. Good for you! You're on the road to success already.

Your son might be a toddler who has recently told you in that determined tone you know means business, "By self, Mom. I do it by self."

Perhaps your son will soon be going off to preschool or kindergarten. You can't help but think, *My baby's leaving the nest.* Half of you looks forward to the break (and the quiet!), but the other half mourns your son going off somewhere—anywhere—without you.

Then there's your nine-year-old, who used to be so close and affectionate but now is backing off a bit. He even asked you the other day to walk a few steps behind him and said, "*Please*, Mom, don't hug me in front of the guys."

And your adolescent son? The one who eats cereal in a bowl you could put a bowling ball in? You're a little tired of hearing a grunt and then a door slam in response to your "How was your day?" Picking up sweaty socks from his jungle of a bedroom isn't your idea of a fun afternoon either.

Then there's your high schooler. The one who shaves but doesn't always use deodorant. Yeah, that one. The same one who gets annoyed when you do the "sniff test" before he walks out the door to school. Sometimes you wonder if you would matter in his life at all if you weren't holding the car keys.

Let's face it. There are times you're really stumped about why your son does what he does. Why he says what he says. And what's he really thinking? You haven't got a clue. Sometimes your son is just such a . . . *boy*.

Boys and girls sure are different, aren't they? I just saw five seventh-grade girls yesterday, talking nonstop and clustered together like a gaggle of geese. The seventh-grade boys? They were strutting like roosters single file behind those girls, acting cooler than cool, high-fiving each other every once in a while in a show of masculine bravado.

Then I caught a glimpse of the second and third graders on the playground. The girls all resembled a covey of quail, traveling in flocks, clucking and hugging. The boys? In the five minutes I watched, three of them were pushing and yelling right in each other's faces, and two more were whacking each other hard on the shoulder. Another boy a little farther down the field got tackled by three other guys in a rough-and-tumble game of football.

Besides the easy-to-see physical trait differences, there are lots of emotional and mental differences too. As a girl yourself, you might not always understand your boy, but he'll always be *your boy*. Your son is altogether different from you, but when it comes to him, you're Mama Bear. May God help anyone who says anything negative about your little cub. They could easily lose an arm.

But you want to know something else? Of all the people in the world, *you*, Mom, make the biggest difference in your son's world. He may not act like it. (In fact, he may act far from it!) Yet when it comes right down to who's the most important to your son, it's you. You see, your son is hiding a secret from you. He'll never reveal it to you straight out, so I'll say it plainly. *Your boy wants to please you.* And that driving need will stay with him for a lifetime.

> *Males aren't nearly as complex as females. But their hearts are just as tender and easily hurt.*

That gives you, Mom, a lot of power in your son's life. You can set your son up for success in life—or failure. You, and only you, can help him understand what it is to be male and how to form healthy relationships with other females. After all, if he doesn't learn that from you, where will he learn it from?

I'll share with you another secret too: males aren't nearly as complex as females. But their hearts are just as tender and easily hurt.

What a Difference a Mom Makes is all about you. It's about your son. It's about the relationship the two of you have right now—and the relationship you *can* have. It's about understanding the male your boy is and helping to craft him into the man you want him to be when he leaves your nest to fly on his own. It's about understanding yourself and why you respond to your son the way you do. And it's about not only weathering the changes in your relationship as your son grows up, but enjoying the fun along the way as well.

The old adage is true: boys *will* always be boys. But honestly, would you want your boy to be any different?

Just don't forget the secret: how much *you matter* in your boy's world.

1

Your Boy Doesn't Need to Wear a Skirt

(But He Does Need a Good Dose of Femininity)

You, Mom, leave an indelible imprint on your child. Here's why.

Honey, what's the matter?" I asked immediately upon hearing my wife's frantic voice on the phone. I was in my office at the time, and I couldn't even decipher what she was saying at first since she was crying and nearly hysterical.

Immediately my heart began to race. One of my kids had to be seriously injured . . . or dead.

Finally my wife blurted out, "It's Kevin!"

Oh no! I thought. I asked, "Did he fall into the pool?" It was my worst nightmare coming to life. My eighteen-month-old son had drowned in our own backyard.

"No," Sande said. More sobs. "It's his tallywhacker."

I wasn't sure I'd heard right. "His tallywhacker?"

"Yeah," she said, "it's *purple*!"

"Purple?" I was really confused now. "What happened? Did somebody hit him?"

"No, he colored it with a magic marker."

I couldn't help it. I burst out laughing. Little Kevin had always shown a predisposition toward art, but this creative endeavor really beat them all.

"What are you laughing about?" Sande asked, horrified.

"Little boys do things like that," I replied. "That's the funniest thing I've ever heard!"

Sande didn't see why it was so funny.

Boys Are Always up to Something

You see, I knew something Sande didn't. Boys will keep you on your toes. I'm a prime example. When I was a boy, my mom hated to do my laundry. Who can blame her? She once reached into my pants pocket and got bit! After hearing a bloodcurdling scream of "Keeeviiin!" I came running and fished out the critters from my pocket. I couldn't understand what the big deal was. After all, I'd gone fishing that day and had just forgotten to remove the crayfish, cricket, grass-hopper, and two salamanders from my jeans.

There's no doubt that boys are not girls. Boys do their nails with their teeth—no expensive manicures needed. Most don't think twice about wearing the same T-shirt they wore yesterday . . . and the day before that . . . even if it does have a few dirt stains or smell a little rank.

Boys spit and burp. They make all sorts of other noises too, like *bbbppssittt* and *vrrooom!* when their toy planes or cars take off at top speed. They like to crash things and knock their sister's blocks down. Such acts are a part of their day. They're rarely quiet, but when they are, you better come running to check things out, because most likely they're up to something. They whistle and tease girls when they like them. They might even push girls or try to wrestle them. (Most girls simply aren't appreciative of such actions. I ought to know, since I tried a few of those moves in my own growing-up years.)

Boys will keep you on your toes.

What Makes Boys So Different from Girls?

What makes boys so different from girls—other than the obvious? Researchers in the journal *Cerebral Cortex* reported a fascinating difference between men and women in regard to the part of the brain that controls visual-spatial abilities and concepts of mental space—skills necessary for tasks such as mathematics and architecture. That area of the brain is about 6 percent larger in men than in women.[1] But does that mean men are smarter? Not necessarily. Men's brains may be larger, but women's contain more brain cells.[2] Also, male and female brains work differently. When men and women perform identical tasks, different areas of their brains light up in response.[3] In addition, females use both hemispheres, while male brain activity is restricted to one side.[4]

Perhaps that's why you sometimes feel you and your son are on opposite sides of the planet—because you truly are. You're able to bounce from brain hemisphere to brain hemisphere, but he's solidly entrenched in one and can see only that side of the equation without your help. Another good reason God almighty created both men and women. We need each other in many ways!

Men tend to focus on the present and the future, and they like to present possibilities whether they're realistic or not. They are often fast moving and risk takers. Contrast that with women, who tend to focus on the present and the past due to their relational abilities, and since they use both sides of their brain, they tend to think more realistically and in detail about tasks that need to be done. As a result, they are usually more cautious and less risk taking. Put the two together and it's easy to see why you and your son will sometimes disagree or even clash.

The more you know about that male critter in your house, the better off you'll be.

But the more you know about that male critter in your house, the better off you'll be.

Boys Are Competitive

Boys are tough. They're competitive. They say things like:

"My dad's stronger than your dad."
"Oh yeah? Well, my dad's got really big muscles. The other day he . . ."
"You think so? Well, last week, *my* dad . . ."

Or like:

"Hey, look at me! I can swing higher!"
"Oh yeah? I can hang upside down!"
"Well, me too!"

Notice all the "I" and "me/my" language that boys use. Now why is that? From the very beginning of their lives, little boys are primed for independence, and that independent edge only grows stronger as they grow older.

Boys are risk takers who don't want anyone else to get ahead of them in life. They've got a drive to be number one and in the fast lane. They're born competi-

> *For boys, it's not just the thing that counts, it's the size of the thing.*

tive. They go after what they want with determination. That's why you'll rarely find guys like me in the slower, right-hand lane of the expressway. We're always the ones zooming to the outside lane to see how far ahead we can get of the next sucker.

Now, my wife? She waits patiently in her lane to get to wherever she wants to go.

For boys, it's not just the thing that counts, it's the size of the thing. That's why if a fourth-grade boy gets a skateboard, his buddy has to get one too . . . but it has to be bigger and badder. It's why the junior high locker room is a difficult and embarrassing place to be. I know about that too. My skinny white body with its sole chest hair wasn't much competition for the boys who already looked like men in every way. And they didn't cut me any slack.

Boys Get Bored—Fast

Within the heart of every boy is an adventurer. Boys like to be on the move. (I can hear some of you saying, "You can say that again! He never stops!") They have wildly different attention spans than girls. They prefer to look at objects for shorter time periods, but they are more active in their

What This Mom Did Right

Ben Carson grew up in abject poverty. He was the son of Sonya, who had dropped out of school in the third grade and married when she was only 13. She and her husband divorced when Ben was only eight, and Sonya cleaned houses, among numerous other jobs, to provide for Ben and his older brother.

When Ben was in fifth grade, he was at the bottom of his class. His mother was determined that both her sons would have a good start in life in spite of their situation, so she took action. She especially wanted them to be good readers (whether they wanted to be or not). Each week she had her sons read two books and write reports on them. This wasn't part of their regular schoolwork but something extra she assigned to them.

Ben was in sixth grade when he found out something intriguing: his mother was basically illiterate. She could barely read the reports her sons turned in to her. But she didn't let anything stop her from encouraging her sons to succeed.

Today Dr. Ben Carson is the top pediatric neurosurgeon (among other roles) at Johns Hopkins University.[5]

attention to that object. Boys are physical beings—they're attracted to the physical. They're not into talking about the details; they're scoping out the details—the way a toy is built, the way a computer runs, or the cute waitress at IHOP.

Boys are more intense and tightly wired, and they're bored much more quickly. Their brains move more rapidly from object to object, which means they can often get the full scope of a project more quickly than girls. But they also take in less sensory information than girls, so they can miss things along the way. That means boys sometimes misinterpret what someone says, because they don't take the time to process both the verbal and the physical cues to see if that person really means what they're saying. That's why sarcastic comments such as "Well, it's about time you took out the trash" are lost on boys. So why not save your own emotional energy and just ask your son in a straightforward manner to take out the trash now?

Boys Are Singularly Focused

When you throw any new information your boy's way, you'll most often hear that famous word: "Huh?" Does this mean your boy is ignoring you? Or that he's completely clueless? No, it means he's deeply focused on the world of whatever he's thinking about, and he isn't able to change his thought track as fast or as often as you can. He's solving a problem, and he can only handle one problem at a time. But no doubt about it—the problem will be solved.

To say that males aren't multitaskers is the understatement of the century.

Males are wired to be singularly focused. When they're doing a task, they're doing just that task—not thinking up their to-do list for the rest of their day like you are. To say that males aren't multitaskers is the understatement of the century. But, Mom, that's why they need you in their world.

I Am King, Hear Me Roar!

Within the heart of every little boy is the need to be king. To conquer and to be the one in charge. To be the one who figures everything out by himself. The lone hero standing on top of the highest rock, sword in hand.

It's why even grown-up men don't ask for directions. They want to figure it out by themselves. It's the challenge of the hunt that drives them. They have the capacity to stop and ask for directions, but they don't want to. They're primed to do the task and believe they can get the job done, even if it's not their natural bent. So why should he need your help, even if you've been driving in circles for an hour and your suggestion to stop is a good one? That's male thinking, as exasperating as it might be to you.

Your son wants to conquer the task, and he doesn't want your help (at least right now—let him get a little more desperate first). It's why your 6-year-old boy tried to take apart your toaster (without your knowledge)—he wanted to figure out how it worked. It's why your 14-year-old is in the living room stomping around—he can't figure out the directions to his new computer game, and he's not about to ask for help. But if you give him a little time to cool down, he'll most likely retackle the task with gusto and figure it out himself. If not, his emotions will have calmed enough that he may even consider asking for help from Dad, the computer guru, or Frank, the next-door-neighbor game whiz.

Boys have the need to be in control and to stay in control. They also have the innate drive to stay on top of the manure pile of life. That's why they work hard and they play hard. *Life belongs to those who get there first, who work hard, who are the fastest, and who stay on top*, boys are primed to think. And they're determined to be the conqueror, the winner.

> Life belongs to those who get there first, who work hard, who are the fastest, and who stay on top, *boys are primed to think.*

That's why your son is likely to tell you about what has gone well for him—at school, in the gym, at work—but isn't as likely to tell you when things go wrong. Doing so goes against his competitive, conqueror-driven nature.

Such an attitude can serve your son well in school, in his career, and in life, but without the balance you bring to the equation, it can be harmful to his relationships.

Your Son's Number One Woman—Guess Who?

Every tough, risk-taking boy needs a good dose of femininity. No, I'm not talking about "getting in touch with his feminine side." For the past several decades, society has been working hard to redefine men's roles and to emphasize the "sensitive" man who is supposed to enjoy cuddling and talkfests, and basically act like a girlfriend would. But is that really who you want your son to be? A girlfriend? Or do you want him to be a real man—one who is determined, honorable, and goal-oriented, but also loving and thoughtful toward the women in his life?

I'm sick of getting in touch with my "feminine self." I like the masculine part just fine, thank you very much.

Frankly, I'm sick of getting in touch with my "feminine self." I like the masculine part just fine, thank you very much. I like channel surfing. I won't apologize for thinking that sex and football are two of the Almighty's and man's greatest inventions (respectively). I don't go to Tupperware parties. I won't eat quiche. I'm comfortable with my testosterone. I like eating with plastic forks—or no forks at all. I don't need a napkin to complete my meal.

Yet anyone who knows me would tell you that this tough guy has a very tender heart toward all his children and his wife, and he is very thankful for all the strong women in his life who are more capable in certain areas than he is.

Are you comfortable with your son? Do you affirm his maleness? More than anything, your son needs for you to appreciate him as a boy and to encourage the masculine qualities you want him to have.

In today's world, some moms are more concerned with increasing a male's sensitivity toward the female population than with affirming male qualities. But such tactics don't really produce the results moms want. Instead, they create confusion—and confused sons tend to make terrible, traumatic choices.

Is it okay to do "girly" things? If a boy has an older sister, like I did, it's only natural for him to sometimes have pretend tea or play with dolls. But there's a huge difference between being comfortable *with* girls and always wanting to act *like* a girl.

No woman wants a sissy for a son. She wants a tough, resilient man who will stand up for others with firm resolve and gentle compassion, and who will have a fierce, protective love and understanding heart for those close to him. Helping your son develop clearly defined gender roles will produce such a mature adult.

But it all starts with you, Mom. In all my years of counseling families and speaking to literally millions of people through radio, television, and seminars, one fact has impressed me as much as anything else: it's the child's relationship with the parent of the *opposite sex* that is most important in families. That means the mother-to-son relationship and the father-to-daughter relationship (for more on this one, see my book *What a Difference a Daddy Makes*).

Mothers leave an indelible imprint on the lives of their sons. Their sons may leave home, graduate from college, get married, and have children of their own, but they'll never stop being Mommy's boy. Although it might be natural to think that the man in your son's life—your husband, your ex-husband, the man who fathered your child, or your boyfriend—would have the most influence on him since they're both males, the opposite is true. *You* influence your son directly and have a much greater impact on the man he will become.

Mothers shape their sons in ways so profound that many men live with their mom's unwritten rules imprinted on them.

That means your son's relationship with you, more than any other relationship, will affect the way he relates to all other females in his life, including bosses, co-workers, subordinates, sisters, wife, and daughters. How you treat him and think of him—and how he treats you and thinks of you—is the key to how he will treat all other females. That means you, Mom, have the edge in picking your own someday daughter-in-law. A man's marriage says far more about his relationship to his mother than it does about his relationship to his father.

You as the mom bring certain qualities and characteristics to the parenting task. If you're married, your testosterone-toting husband brings an entirely different perspective and approach. He may be a lot tougher on your son than you are because he expects more out of him (especially if your son is a firstborn). And you may be a lot more tender. Sometimes the reverse is true, though it's not as likely since Mama Bear is always protective of her cubs. If you're a single parent and you're trying to be mom *and* dad, there's good news: you don't have to be both. (What a relief, huh?) Just be his *mom*, and you can heap blessings on him for a lifetime. (For more on that, see chapter 10.)

The more you understand about this unique mother-son relationship, the better you'll be able to help repair a damaged heart or strengthen an already healthy relationship both now and in the future.

What Your Boy Needs Most from You

No matter what age your boy is, there are three things he needs most from you.

He needs to be respected. Your son may be 13 and have recently dyed his hair blue, but he still needs to know that you respect who he is at his core, instead of merely looking

What He Needs from You

- To be respected.
- To be needed.
- To be fulfilled.

at his exterior and thinking how he'll embarrass you in front of your friends. Keep in mind that little secret I shared with you: your boy *wants* to please you. You're his mama, the most important person in his world . . . even if he is asking you to walk a couple steps behind him and his friends. Your son needs you to believe he is a capable, worthy human being. He needs to know he is important in your world, and not just another thing to take care of or clean up after. He longs for acceptance, a sense of belonging, and companionship from *you*. No one else will do.

He needs to be needed. Again, your boy wants to please you. He just may not know how to do it. If you look too capable (at times the multitasking abilities of you moms can be incredibly intimidating to us men), he may not risk trying to help. Why not give him some ways to help? You'll do yourself a favor too.

"Fletcher, would you mind moving the couch for me? I'd love to vacuum under there tonight, but it's too heavy for me to move."

Your sometimes surly, hormone-laden 15-year-old will leap to help, flexing his muscles as he does. If you play your cards right, you might even get him to vacuum! Why? Because you've shown him that you need him. He's not just another piece of furniture but a needed member of the family.

Think of ways to include your son, no matter his age, as an active member of the family. Two-year-olds can do a great job putting away their own toys. "Sam, Mommy would love it if you would pick up your toys and put them in your toy box. Will you do that while I make macaroni and cheese for dinner?" Bet that toy box will be filled in record time. You may not be able to close the lid—after all, your son may not do things exactly the way you'd do them—but in the long run, does that really matter? Or is it more important that your son felt needed?

It's especially important that sons feel needed around the house, since males tend to live as islands. They have fewer friends than women do, so they have fewer relationships. If they don't learn to help and relate at home while they are growing up, who will teach them? Your daughter-in-law and grandchildren will someday thank you for your efforts. See how influential you are?

Think of ways to include your son, no matter his age, as an active member of the family.

Your son needs to be needed not just by anyone. He needs to be needed by you. So let him be a boy. Let him be a conqueror, let him compete, let him problem solve in his own way (even if you immediately see the answer). When you do so, you encourage your son to further his efforts and abilities to help not only himself but others as well. Your son needs to know he has a solid place in your world, in your home, and in your heart.

He needs to be fulfilled as a man. That includes knowing who he is—specifically as a male, what makes him unique, and how he should relate to women. No one can teach him more about what women want and how they deserve to be treated than you, a woman. If you have a husband who's a wonderful daddy, your son has a great start for male role models. Uncles and other close male family friends can also fulfill that role for a growing boy. But what your boy needs from you is your acceptance of his masculinity.

You often hear, "That's my boy!" from dads, but how often do you hear that statement from moms? Your boy needs to know that he belongs to you, that you think he's special just as he is, and that you appreciate his maleness—the ways he thinks differently from you, the times he uses his physical strength to shovel snow and mow grass, the way he looks out for his younger sister at school on the playground. Affirm his maleness, and you'll have a boy who will be eager to help around the house and will go the extra mile for you when needed.

Most of all, teach him how to see through your eyes what it's like to be a woman. Explain why whacking a girl on the head won't gain her interest or her respect, but smiling, engaging her in conversation, and offering her a Snickers bar will go a long way toward friendship. Teach him manners—how to use a napkin, to say "please" and "thank you," to answer the phone politely, and to start a conversation with a girl. Explain, age appropriately, how girls and boys are different in both thinking and needs, and how wonderful and exciting a relationship can be. After all, who better than you to explain how girls think and feel, since you happen to own the very same equipment as your son's future girlfriend?

Don't ever allow your son to treat you in any way that debases you as a female. If you do, you are setting up patterns in him that will negatively impact every female he has a relationship with, as well as the next generation (if he has children).

You don't need to put a skirt on your son or teach him to play with dolls in order to make him able to relate to his sisters and his someday girlfriend or wife. But you do need to explain clearly to your son what a woman wants from a man and what she needs to feel fulfilled.

What You Can Do

- Let your boy be a boy.
- Let him conquer and compete. (He'll have to in order to survive in a man's world anyway.)
- Show him how much he is needed in your family.
- Teach him how females deserve to be treated.

Remember the top three needs for a man? To be respected, to be needed, and to be fulfilled. Well, the top three needs for a woman are quite different: affection, honest and open communication, and commitment to family. Through your own actions in your home and your interactions with your son, you can help your son learn inherently how to meet these three needs. And that's an indelible imprint that will last a lifetime and rocket him to success in all his relationships.

Mama Bear and Cubby Leman

I was always close to my mother when I was growing up. Even during the years when kids have a hard time talking to their parents, I could talk to my mother about anything—including girls and sex. My mother was a straight talker. I also knew she loved me. And no matter what others said about me, she believed in and expected the best of me.

My mother had a lot of stresses in her life. We were poor. We didn't have a car, only a panel truck my dad used in his small dry-cleaning business. It didn't even have a passenger seat, just a driver's seat. I sat on the dry-cleaning bags on the floor of the front seat of that truck. There were no seat belts in those days.

My dad was a drinker. He embarrassed me and my mom more times than I can count. The most money he ever made in one year was $12,000—for a family of five. When his small business floundered, Mom went to work full-time as a registered nurse and often worked all night. One of my most vivid memories is of watching her walk through two feet of snow at seven o'clock in the morning. She was coming down our street in Buffalo, New York, after working the night shift at the hospital.

How I loved my mother. And it was always clear Mama Bear loved me, my brother, and my sister. In the midst of all the hard work, she took time to go fishing with me. We'd walk to the creek half a mile from our house and catch fish. She'd celebrate each of my catches as if they were the most spectacular ones any boy had ever gotten!

It was always clear Mama Bear loved me, my brother, and my sister.

My mother was my champion, even when, in the world's eyes, I was a failure—the dumber-than-mud kid who couldn't finish consumer mathematics (even the girl who ate glue did), flunked Latin three times, and never "got" chemistry at all. I took elementary algebra so many times I could have declared it my major. I was headed nowhere—fast.

Little did I know until much later that my mother often prayed, "God, please have Kevin bring home just one C on his report card to show me there is *something* there." She was often at school more than I was—talking to teachers who were constantly saying, "If Kevin would only apply himself . . ."

My mother continued to pray when I was thrown out of the one college that had managed to accept me, and I became a janitor. During that time of trying to "find myself," I took a

night course in geology at the nearby University of Arizona
. . . and promptly flunked it. The next semester I took it again
. . . and flunked it again.

Then something miraculous happened. I met a woman
who believed in me just like my mom did: Sande, a nurse's
aide. I fell head over heels in love with her. She reintroduced
me to church and to the God my mom believed in and had
raised me to believe in.

My life did a 180. I went back to school full-time even while
I continued working as a janitor. The first semester back, I
passed all my classes and was even put on the honors list. I still
remember staring in shock at my name on that list. Imagine
my greater shock when I was asked to report to the dean.

My first response? "I didn't do nothin' wrong!" (It was
a learned response, believe me.) I was scared. My little-boy
thinking told me, *Last time I saw a dean, he threw me out
of college.*

I went to see him anyway. And you know what? He told me
I had won university scholarship honors and that the school
was going to pay for my tuition the next semester.

My dear mother finally had something to be proud of, after
a very long wait. I credit my success and who I have become
now to this woman who believed in me, even when believing
was such a long stretch of faith that it looked impossible.

Even though Mama Bear May Leman is now in heaven,
this Cubby still feels the warmth of her love and belief sur-
rounding my life.

Mama Bear Sande and Cubby Kevin II

Remember Sande's shock at Kevin II coloring his tallywhacker
purple?

Any less-brave mom would have hidden all the magic markers after that event. But not my Sande. Seeing his artistic ability and wanting to channel it into something more helpful, Sande encouraged Kevin in the field of art. (She's artistic herself but doesn't give herself enough credit.) When Kevin was a little guy, Sande always had in her purse a new crayon, a colored pencil, and some paper to draw on if there was any waiting time wherever they went. She even allowed him to decorate his own bedroom in New York. We still call it the Aladdin room since characters of that movie are sketched all over the walls.

Kevin has always been an idea person. He can't spell worth a darn, but he's fantastically creative. His major in college? Art. Now he's a world-class artist, and he works for one of the top-rated television shows as a creative writer. He's even won two Emmys. And who does he credit with kicking off his artistic abilities and encouraging them? Dear ol' Mom.

Also, the way Sande taught him to relate to the opposite sex had girls in his preschool lining up to give little Kevin a hug. Today, this same charming personality has gained him footholds and friendships with both males and females in the upper echelons of Hollywood. Anyone who knows Kevin has nothing but good to say about him, his creativity, his passion for getting the job done, and his integrity.

That's my son. That's Sande's son.

And Sande gets 95 percent of the credit for it. (Hey, I have to give myself just a sliver of credit too.)

So, Mom, encourage the best in your son. Let him be who he is—that competitive, go-for-the-goal thinker and doer. Teach him to treat you and other females with the respect you deserve, but don't put a skirt on him. He doesn't have the legs for it anyway.

2

Planning
Your Toddler's Wedding

Want a boy who will be a great husband for your
future daughter-in-law and a great father for
your grandchildren? Here's how. (By the way,
did you know that you also play a large role in
picking your future daughter-in-law?)

Minutes ago, as I was driving along an Arizona road near a dry riverbed, a group of javelinas crossed the road right in front of me. These wild pigs tend to travel in herds. There certainly was a grandma and grandpa in the group. They were huge and moved slowly. A lot of others were more normal sized. And then there was Mama Javelina. No doubt she was the mom. Eight little pigs were following her as close as they could in perfect single-file marching order.

37

(That mama had them well trained, as only mamas can do.) Then one more little pig caught my eye. She must have been only eight inches long. And you know where she was? Following right *under* her mama. Talk about protection—she was right under her mama's forelegs, running with her little legs as fast as she could to keep up.

That mama javelina was certainly a protector. She was protecting all her babies, especially the smallest one.

From day one, Mama Bear always protects her young. But just like in the wild, there's also a time when she has to say, "Okay, now you're on your own. Go get your own territory." And isn't that what growing up is all about?

Little Cubby Wasn't Always So Cute . . .

At a family reunion, my cousin Eleanor told me a story about my growing-up years. She and her husband were young marrieds when they came to visit my family. As they walked through the door, I punched Eleanor in the stomach as a greeting.

"I wanted to choke you to death right there in the vestibule of your home," Eleanor told me. "But what really got me going is that your mother, who had seen it all happen, thought you were so cute."

That wasn't the only time I got away with murder.

I was probably four or five at the time. And no, I wasn't cute; I was obnoxious. In fact, if I saw some little kid do that to somebody today, I'd apply an ether cloth to the kid's nose and he'd take an instant nap.

But that wasn't the only time I got away with murder. I knew well how to use my baby-of-the-family wiles to get away with a lot.

My own behavior came back to haunt me when my son, Kevin, was young. At last I understood how my mother would have thought I was cute (in spite of my detestable behavior) when my own wife responded the same way—not once but numerous times. When Kevin was little, he got obnoxious from time to time, like every kid does. But when he was in the midst of doing something obnoxious, with the neighbor watching, did Sande chide him? No. She said (and I quote), "Isn't he *adorable?*"

There were stars of love in her eyes and a smile on her lips. Now that's the mother-son filtering system. Nobody touches Cubby Bear except Mama Bear, and he's always cute. Amazing how he can look that way through your rose-colored lenses.

But just because he's cute to you doesn't mean he's cute to anyone else. There's love, and then there's discipline—you can't have one without the other and still come out with a well-adjusted, healthy, balanced adult.

Just because he's cute to you doesn't mean he's cute to anyone else.

Mom, you have a great gift in this little guy or big guy. He's moldable clay in your fingers. You set him up for success or failure in life—developmentally, emotionally, sexually, mentally, and spiritually.

So how do you get started, or how do you go on from where you are now if you're already driving down the parenting road?

Start with the End in Mind

Dream a bit with me. Look down the road 5 years, then 10 years, then 15 years, then 20 years. Who do you want your

---

Where Do You Want Your Son to Be:

- 5 years from now?
- 10 years from now?
- 15 years from now?
- 20 years from now?

Do a little dreaming, then make some notes. You'll be glad you did.

---

son to be? What do you want his relationships to be like? His life to be like? Take time to scribble down your ideas. I'll still be here. . . .

Okay, got your list in hand? Take a good look at it. Read each one carefully. If that list is where you want your son to be at those milestones, how will you get there?

Dr. Stephen Covey, bestselling author and business consultant, says that if you want to get to your destination, you have to "start with the end in mind." That means, in Lemanese, you work your way backward.

If you want a son who is kind, you emphasize kindness. If you want a son who is responsible, you give him age-appropriate responsibility and hold him accountable. If you want a child who has a good work ethic, you set the ground rules at home. If you want your child to enjoy time with you, start now in setting aside unpressured time to spend with him instead of allowing your family to be pulled into the constant rat race of activity.

If you want your son to become a healthy, well-adjusted adult—the kind of adult you can be proud of, a wonderful husband, a loving daddy—how do you go about it?

I'm Getting Married in the Morning . . .

As the old wedding song says in the movie *My Fair Lady*, "I'm getting married in the morning. Ding dong! The bells are gonna chime." Someday, Mom, your baby will get married. (After he grows up, of course.) When he does, what kind of woman will he marry? Will she be sweet, strong-minded, happy, and secure? Or will she be manipulative, changeable, moody, and insecure?

Did you know that right now you are helping to pick that woman for him?

Sure you are!

The flowers, the beautiful gown, the reception dinner—all that will be left up to the bride's family. But you are helping to choose your son's life partner *right now*, even if your son is only a toddler, a far cry from getting married.

How can that be?

By what happens in your home, you are setting your son up to marry a certain kind of woman. Did you know that no matter what your relationship with your son is like, he'll tend to marry a woman like you?

Surprised? Well, it's true.

You are helping to choose your son's life partner right now.

Because he's used to the way you treat him, your son is likely to marry someone who is just like you—even if he thinks he won't.

Take Aaron, for instance, whose mom is a very overprotective woman who didn't let him stray far from his apron strings. He was thrilled when he met Judy in college. She seemed like the perfect woman for him—smart, a music major who wanted to teach piano from her home, and even able to cook. But a few months into their marriage, she was constantly calling him to see where he was and when he'd be home, and she'd fuss if he was a few minutes late.

"Dr. Leman, I just can't handle it anymore," Aaron confessed. "I said I'd *never* marry someone like my mother, and Judy's just like her. I'm so trapped. I'm losing my mind."

Contrast him with Mark, who has been happily married to Tammy for 12 years. Tammy and Mark's mom get along like two peas in a pod. You can frequently find them shopping together and swapping recipes. Although Tammy works part-time and Mark's mom didn't work outside the home, the two couldn't be more alike in temperament.

"My mom has a great sense of humor," Mark says, "and so does Tammy. And they both are great at creating fun without spending much money. I always admired that about my mom. We grew up really poor, but we never felt poor because Mom had such a great attitude. With my mom and Tammy, man, I've got the best of everything."

Did you catch that? Your attitude, Mom, makes all the difference in your son's life both now and in the future! That puts a new spin on things, doesn't it? What an encouragement to keep on doing what you're doing well and to work on what's not going so well!

Now's the right time to check out your relationship with your son. Do you allow your son to get away with being disrespectful to you? It's so easy to let him off the hook when he bats those baby blues at you after getting in trouble. And then you start thinking about all those hours you spent in labor with him—when you saw the product at the end, wow! You were in love. Just remembering such an occasion deflates your ire. Suddenly you've forgotten what you were so angry about.

But, Mom, don't do it! Insist on respect in your house, and model it. You're a strong, smart woman, and you can't afford to be weak in this area. Too much lies in the balance. If you let your son run all over you, who do you think is next? His wife, of course. He'll not only marry a woman he can run over (since he's got that down pat with you), he'll try the same tactics on her that worked on you when he was growing up.

So why not create a boy who will be a great husband for your future daughter-in-law? A boy who will be a great father for your grandchildren?

It all starts with your relationship with your son and your awareness of his world.

Be Aware of Your Son's World

Raising kids today is a little scary. Drugs are prolific. Many high schools today have to have weapon-screening systems, yet guns and knives still manage to make their way into the classroom. Kids are angry and disenfranchised. Young children are diagnosed with depression. Fights break out on the playground. Your son competes every day with other boys who are bigger than him, stronger than him, and tougher than him. Some days he wins and some days he loses. He might even come home with a black eye. On top of that, if he's just discovering the wonderful world of girls, he's concerned about his acne, his looks, the size of his biceps, and a host of other things. He's also facing the challenges of a peer group who goads him to "get laid." After all, "everybody does it."

Your boy lives in a tough world. No wonder sometimes you can get only grunts out of him after days like those. And if he doesn't measure up in some way—he's small physically or too frail—the world can be extra tough.

Thirty years later, Jason still remembers vividly a day at the end of eighth grade. He was one of those "wimpy" kids the boys always picked on. "I had a lot of girls as friends, because they didn't see me as someone to date," he says. One day, the guys ganged up on him in the locker room, stripped him down to his undershorts, and hog-tied him to the flagpole outside the front of the school for all to see. "I thought I'd die of embarrassment," he says.

But though he remembers the event, it doesn't haunt him anymore, because he had one sharp cookie of a mother. Mama Andrea decided enough was enough. (This was one of a series of events that had happened to her son, and the principal had just laughed about it, saying boys would be boys.) She marched into school the next day, said her son would not be attending there the next year, and explained that she was there to collect his end-of-the-year tests and would administer them herself. Then she went home, made a lot of phone calls, and enrolled her son in a smaller high school known for its technical and computer opportunities—something Jason was very interested in.

Jason flourished at that school and finished with top grades. He also found good buddies in like-minded (and like-bodied) boys. Today he's one of the three top executives at a large computer firm. All compliments of his mama, he claims, grinning.

You see, Mom, there's a time when you butt out and let your child handle his own problems. But there are other times when you need to step in and take action. Mama Andrea was a strong woman who let her son handle his problems—up to a point. Then she stepped in like Mama Bear.

There's a time when you butt out and let your child handle his own problems. But there are other times when you need to step in and take action.

You may be holding your six-month-old son in your arms right now. Or you might be waving your son out the door to go to college. But the more you're aware of his world and the risks involved with that world, the more you can help.

Keep an Eye on His Behavior

Is your son the kind of child you can take anywhere and you know he'll behave? Let's say he had a day off from school. Could you take him to work with you without worrying about him embarrassing you? Does your toddler pitch a fit when you don't buy his favorite candy at the grocery store, or does he sit quietly in the cart and "help" you pick out the groceries? Does your adolescent stomp off when he doesn't get his way? Is your just-turned-teenager acting weird (even for him)?

It's natural for kids to get angry, but they need to learn how to deal with that anger when things go wrong or they don't get what they want. It's natural for adolescents to take longer in the bathroom as they begin to figure out and explore their changing bodies. And it's also natural for teenagers to want a little more time to themselves, to sleep more (their bodies are changing so rapidly that they need the sleep), and to want a little more privacy as they try to figure out this new world they've stepped into. As Anne Hathaway says in *The Princess Diaries*, "I'm still waiting for normal body parts to arrive!" But if your son's temperament does a 180—your normally bubbly 8-year-old becomes withdrawn and morose and remains that way, or your 13-year-old starts locking his bedroom door—then it's time to investigate why these changes are taking place.

Teach Him Manners and How to Interact with Girls

There's nothing more annoying to me than a kid who can't say "thank you" without his mom prompting him for the zillionth time: "Now, William, say 'thank you.'" And William's in fourth grade!

Babies don't come out of the womb saying "please" and "thank you." They have to be taught the niceties of life, and the sooner the better. The other day I drove a group of high school girls from school to their homes, and you know what? Not a single one said "thank you" except Lauren, my own daughter! That was an eye-opener.

Your son won't be born with manners. He has to be taught. Otherwise he'll do what comes naturally—he'll burp at the table, yell raucously inside the house, try to impress girls with his spitting ability, and get in an all-out war with his buddies to see who can make the loudest bodily noise. There's a place for letting boys be boys, and there's a time when they need to be gentlemen. Teach your son to know the difference, and he'll be way ahead of the game when it comes to pursuing that girl he has his eye on.

Teach your child that kindness matters greatly. Your son should be taught the golden rule: do unto others as you would have others do unto you. And that rule should be followed in your home by all members of the family. If you want a son who will give to the poor and others in need, model that in your home. Get involved with Meals on Wheels, deliver groceries to a neighbor family in need, serve at a local soup kitchen on weekends, befriend a boy in need. Such activities will foster gratefulness in your son for what he has instead of a drive to get what he doesn't have.

Make sure your son pulls his own weight in domestic jobs, even if he is the only boy in the family. Just because he's a boy doesn't mean he shouldn't help with dishes, throw in a load of laundry, and learn how to cook dinner. Those are basic life skills for living on your own, and the boy who knows how to do them and does them for himself will be much more appreciative of a wife who may share those tasks with him down the road.

Boys also don't naturally know how to relate to girls. They need to be taught because, frankly, boys are *not* girls. So how could they know how girls think and feel?

That's where you step in, Mom. Who better for your son to practice on than you, a girl? You'll be a lot more forgiving of his mistakes than a potential date will. So teach your son that girls like to be treated kindly, gently, sensitively. They are impressed if a guy can enter their world through conversation, such as, "I noticed you were at soccer tryouts the other day. Are you interested in getting on a team, or did you go to support a friend?" That tells the girl that she was noticed and that your son is treating her like a real, live person, not just a good-looking chick.

> *Boys are not girls. So how could they know how girls think and feel?*

Clue your son in, age appropriately, about a female's cycles—why she has them, that she may be a little crabby at certain times of the month, and that she needs to be treated more tenderly during such times. (Who better to explain cramps and how they make you feel than you?) Your future daughter-in-law will really stand up and be your cheerleader for paving the way for her!

When your son begins to get interested in dating, who better to practice on than you? So go on a date with your son. Have him treat you like he would a date: pick you up at the door, make conversation, acknowledge any parents in the house with a smile, say he'll take good care of their daughter, open the house door for you, open the car door for you, etc. Have him make all the arrangements for where he's taking you (movie? dinner? skating party?), just as he would for a real date. If your son is going to be uncomfortable, why not let that be with you first so he'll be more confident on that first date with a girl? But give your son a break and don't act like his date in public, because that would embarrass him.

Above all, teach your son to treat his own sexuality with care and to treat his date with the same care and respect. The question to solidify in his mind is: *If Mom was watching me, would I be comfortable with my actions?* Hormones run wild, and they can run wilder if there's no check on them. Teach your son the importance of keeping his penis in his pants and keeping his roving hands to himself. Dating is meant for two people to get to know each other, to see if a future relationship is possible. But that relationship is short-circuited as soon as sex enters the picture.

These days, so many young people aren't virgins when they get married. If you teach your son the wisdom of waiting until his wedding night to share himself sexually with his bride, your son will be a prize catch indeed.

Make Your Home a Place of Connection

What kind of home do you have? Is it a safe place—a place of peace and calm? Or is it a place of tension? When your son walks through the door, is it a relief for him to come home or just another place where he gets nagged?

Have you emphasized mutual respect? You for your son? Your son for you? And siblings for each other? Is it an environment where your son knows that even on a grumpy day, you still love him and he is welcome to find comfort in your arms? Believe it or not, your 17-year-old tough guy who got dumped by his girlfriend may not act like he wants a hug, but he could be aching for one, or at least a few kind words such as, "I'm sorry, son." His little-boy heart is just as tender and hurt as when he used to sit on your lap and tell you about

What Your Son Needs from You

- Unconditional acceptance
- Belonging to your family group
- To know that you consider him competent and capable

his boo-boos. (Hint: Food really is the way to a guy's heart, especially your growing teenager's. The aroma of some warm chocolate chip cookies to welcome him home takes the edge off any bad day. And for those of you who don't bake, don't worry—there's always the Pillsbury Doughboy waiting for you in the refrigerated section of the supermarket.)

It's all about connection, and a home isn't a home without connection—it's a hotel, where people come and go and can eat from a breakfast buffet every once in a while if they wish.

If you want a boy who will grow up to be a wonderful husband and loving father, who is strong in himself and in his self-worth yet understanding and sensitive toward others, focus on three areas in his growing-up years. If you could ask any kid what matters most to them, you would most likely hear in their answer something to do with acceptance, belonging, or competence.

Acceptance

Go back a few years, Mom, to those painful days in adolescence when you longed to be accepted for who you were. Maybe you didn't have breasts yet and everybody else in your sixth-grade gym class did, so you always faked having to go to the restroom so you could change in privacy in a stall. You might not have had the kind of body that turned the heads of the junior-high boys like some of your girlfriends did, but when you got home, you could always count on a mean game of soccer with your two brothers. And they didn't care that you didn't have breasts.

Acceptance is everything in a child's life. Remember the secret from earlier? Your son *wants* to please you. He longs for your approval. He may never put that in words, but inside he's saying, "Do you think I'm okay? Just like I am?"

Your son will live up to your unwritten expectations for him. Do you portray by your words and actions, "Yeah, you're doing a good job. You know, you're a pretty great kid. I'm proud of you, and you should be proud of yourself. I think you can accomplish anything you put your mind to, so how 'bout it? What's next that you want to try?" If so, you're encouraging your son to fly to the moon! The sky's the limit in what you believe he can accomplish. But the key here is that his accomplishments need to be *his*, not yours (like doing or finishing a project for him). That's how you establish healthy self-worth.

Or are your words and actions saying, "You've got to be the dumbest kid I've ever seen. You always interrupt me in the middle of what I'm doing, and sometimes you're just plain stupid"? If so, your child will have low self-worth and think he can never accomplish anything. If your child is a procrastinator, take a good look at yourself. Is it because your son knows he can never be good enough for you, so why would he even start the project or bother to do anything you ask because you'll just tell him how to do it better? If so, check your own expectations. Are they too high for the abilities of your son? If your son is a B and C student and you expect him to get all As, it shouldn't surprise you if he's not completing or turning in his homework. After all, if he knows he won't get an A anyway, why bother? He'll never be good enough for you.

Did you know that your son will fly high for days on just one compliment from you? That's because you're so important in his world. But that compliment has to be sincere. Your son's smart enough to know the difference. If you praise him by saying, "Oh, buddy, you're just the greatest in everything you do!" your son will look at you cock-eyed and think, *Yeah, right. I know that's not true. Jake just scored a goal on me yesterday, I got a D on my social studies test, and my best friend thinks I'm a jerk because I said something dumb in math class.* But if you encourage your son by saying, "Hey, buddy, I noticed that you studied really long for your science test.

> *Your son will fly high for days on just one compliment from you.*

And look at that, you got an A-! I know science is hard for you, and you pulled out all the stops to study for that one. Wow, that's so great," that'll make him grin and he'll high-five himself. You can bet he'll study hard for the next science test with that kind of encouragement.

You see, praise and encouragement are very different. Praise is pointed at the person: "Well, look at *you. You* are so great." Encouragement is pointed at the act: "Well, look at *what* you did. That's really wonderful." Praise is empty; it doesn't last. What happens when your kid isn't the best? Your son isn't dumb enough to fall for that, so he just tunes you out because he knows you're faking it. *Boy, I must be a loser if she can't come up with one good thing to say about what I've done,* your son thinks. *So why bother?* But encouragement? That lasts a lifetime. It propels your son to risk trying something new (even if he fails), hones his creativity, and also opens his eyes to the possibilities of who he might become if he tries.

But does accepting your son mean that you like everything he does? No. Unconditional acceptance doesn't mean looking the other way when he does something dumb or gets himself in trouble. Acceptance means loving your son as your son, no matter what he does, but continuing to hold him accountable for his actions.

If your son feels accepted by you at home, he won't go looking for that acceptance elsewhere. If he finds it in a peer group, that's great—it's just added to the unconditional acceptance he gets at home. But if your son doesn't get that at home, then the peer group becomes extremely *more* important and can lead him into trouble.

Belonging

"My son Hank was at a new friend's house recently," a mom told me, "when it turned into a big beer fest. Hank's only 14, so he couldn't drive, and he couldn't reach me on my cell to come get him. One of the guys at the party kept pressuring him to drink a beer. At first, Hank just said, 'No thanks.' The guy pressed again: 'Come on. It's just a beer. What are you, a wimp?' Hank shook his head. 'No, I'm not a wimp,' he said. 'I'm a Clark, and we Clarks don't drink. But I'll take a Coke if you have one.' I'm so proud of my son!"

That mom had reason to be proud. Her son stood up against strong peer pressure and didn't cave in. And because he stood firm, it's not likely those same guys will pressure him again. Even more, that mom was happy to find out that her child had aligned himself with her family. "He was proud to be a Clark," she said. "That just blew me away!"

Every child needs a place to belong. What group would you rather your son belong to? His peer group? A gang? Or you and your family?

Your boy needs a group to identify with—a "shared ID." If he doesn't find it with you, he'll go elsewhere. So make sure your home is a place of belonging, where everyone gets their say in family decisions. Where everyone's opinion is respected. Go to each other's activities *together*. Have family dinners (and not in front of the blaring TV). Do something old-fashioned—talk to each other.

> *What group would you rather your son belong to? His peer group? A gang? Or you and your family?*

The need to belong somewhere is deeply ingrained in each of us. If there's no sense of belonging, there's no relationship. And without a relationship, what you say and what you do mean nothing. It would be like pulling in a guy off the street and putting him in charge of your family, for all his rules would mean to your son.

But establish that sense of belonging, and you set your son up for success for a lifetime.

Competence

Want an adult male who tackles with gusto any project he's given? Who, when stumped, will look at all angles of a project and won't give up until he's put the challenge to rest? Then treat your son as if he's competent—no matter his age. Your 3-year-old is fully capable of cleaning out your Tupperware closet and stacking like items together. Your 9-year-old can help your 4-year-old learn how to tie his shoes. Your 13-year-old can make a box of macaroni and cheese for his younger siblings as you're doing the laundry. Your 16-year-old who has a license is fully capable of making a run to the grocery store or post office for you.

Give your son some responsibility and watch him fly. *Hey, Mom says I can do it*, he thinks. *And I will!* Again, it goes back to expectations. Expect the best, and you'll most often get the best.

So treat your son as part of the family. After all, he lives in a home, not a hotel, so he should pitch in to help. The more tasks he does, the more confident he gets in doing them. As a result, his competence level increases, and he can do more and more on his own.

Expect the best, and you'll most often get the best.

Never do anything for your children that they can do for themselves. By giving your son age-appropriate responsibility, you are helping him get ready to move out into the adult world as a healthy, functioning member of society.

Remember That Nobody's Perfect

Nobody's perfect, and everybody has bad moments and bad days. Some even last longer than days. Kids can be dumber than mud, and your son will do his share of dumb things. Like trying to see if he can fly like a bird off the roof of the garage. Or sticking his tongue to the playground swing pole on a dare on a 15-degrees-below-zero day. Or saying, "Oh yeah?" to the neighborhood bully, then realizing he can't run fast enough.

Boys are experimental, and they'll try anything, including putting snakes under their sister's pillow and a cricket in your teacup. They'll pick up nails from a construction site, build their own hodgepodge tree house, and put up a sign that says No Girls Allowed.

No matter how good of a parent you are, your child will sometimes get in trouble. About a month ago I got a phone call from Deana, who was in shock. Her fifth-grade "good boy," Trey, had just been caught throwing a rock at another kid's head, and he was in the principal's office. When she asked him why he did it, he simply shrugged and said, "I don't know. All the other guys had rocks in their hands, and they were throwing them. But they didn't get caught. I did."

After Deana got over her shock, she realized it was time for what I call a "teachable moment"—the time when your child's ears are open to whatever you have to say. So she had a long discussion with her son about how important it is to think for yourself instead of just following the rules of the crowd. It was the perfect time for such a discussion, since Trey is going into junior high next year, where peer pressure will be upped and his power of resistance will be tested even further.

When your kid messes up, let him live with the consequences. For instance, Trey had to apologize in the principal's office to the boy he threw the stone at. Deana, the principal, and Trey also agreed that he would lose his recess time for a week. He'd have to sit quietly in the library and read a book during that time. That was a tough punishment for an on-the-go boy who loved recess and hated reading. But interestingly, during that time the librarian introduced him to fantasy—swashbuckling soldiers and dragons—and Trey learned that books aren't so bad after all.

Since the event had happened at school and the punishment was being carried out at school and was agreed on by all, Deana decided that no further actions needed to be taken at home. So when Trey got home, she didn't continually remind him of his mistake. But they did have a lot of discussions about fantasy books!

What This Mom Did Right

Celebrity superstar Usher calls his mom, Jonnetta Patton, "the total package" and "my everything." For a while, she acted as his manager until they decided mutually to "give [my mother] the ultimate compliment—to retire her to be a full-time grandmother. My mother and I decided to change her situation, together," he reports.

Has their relationship always been easy? No. He says that his mom can be aggressive sometimes, and she's up-front if she doesn't like something. But he also states that his mother was always there for him growing up and when he entered the music business.[1]

So, Mom, give your son the freedom to fail while he's still in the nest. How you handle his failures is so much more important than how you handle his victories. It's easy to be critical, to pick at flaws, to harp continually on mistakes he's made. But think of it this way: If your words were directed at yourself, how would you feel? Shamed? Embarrassed? Or would the gentleness of your words and actions make you say, "You know, you're right. I shouldn't have done that. That was stupid. So thanks for pointing me on the right path. I'll do better next time. Will you help me?"

Your treatment sets up your son's self-worth. *Am I a worthwhile human being or not? What will happen if I mess up?* Yet the question isn't *if*, it's *when*, because we will all mess up. But when we do, God almighty himself gives us unconditional love and the opportunity to change our direction. How can you do less for your own son?

Your unconditional love will speak volumes to your son and will help to forge a close bond with him both now and in the future. But always remember that love and discipline are a team—you can't have one without the other. Holding a child accountable for his actions is one thing; browbeating him for mistakes is quite another.

Realize That You Too Make Mistakes

Sande and I have raised five children—with all of them now out of the nest. We've made our share of mistakes, and so will you. I remember vividly one day when my angry daughter said to me, "You know what you ought to do? *Read your own book!*" Oh boy, she nailed me.

Mistakes are part of the journey called parenting. But the good news is that you can learn from them. You can improve your parenting, building responsible kids and joyful, long-lasting relationships with them.

You'll never be a perfect parent. It's not possible. But you can step up to the plate and commit yourself to being the best parent you can be. It won't be easy. It won't always be fun. But I guarantee you, it'll be worth it.

Give your son the freedom to fail while he's still in the nest.

Every time my family gathers together—there are 12 of us now that 3 of our children are married and we have 2 grandchildren—Sande and I look at each other and smile. We've raised kids who like us and each other and enjoy hanging out together whenever possible. And in between, we're keeping Verizon in the style she's accustomed to with our nonstop phone calls to each other. It's all about relationship—connecting hearts and interweaving lives—and we go out of our way to keep that a priority in the Leman family.

When you mess up, apologize to your son. Be straightforward about what you did wrong and ask for his forgiveness. Don't let pride hamper your developing relationship. Say, "Son, when I did X, X, and X, I was wrong. Will you please forgive me?" When you humble yourself to say "I'm sorry" to your son, you're giving him the tools to further hone his

What You Can Do

- Think not just about now but down the road as well.
- Teach him to be kind and courteous, and you'll heap blessings on his head.
- Make your home a *home*—not a hotel.

future relationships. You're role modeling healthy forgiveness instead of seething resentment.

And I can't think of a single daughter-in-law who wouldn't thank you profusely for that!

Ding Dong! The Bells Are Gonna Chime

Start with the end in mind, and you'll be amazed at the progress you make.

The bride, the flowers, and the wedding gown won't be the only beautiful things you see the day your son gets married. You'll see that shimmering, near-teary look of wonder on your son's face as he watches his bride walk down the aisle. And you can be sure a similar look will be on your face. Bet you'll have a wad of Kleenex to boot.

You see, you already know the secret. *You* are the one who helped pick that wonderful mate for your son. By focusing on acceptance, belonging, and competence in your home and while your son was growing up, you set him up for success not only in business relationships but in all his relationships—especially this most important one. Sure, he might have gone through the process of dating her, but you know that you set him up to pick just the right gal. You also taught him kindness, respect, understanding, and sensitivity toward how women want to be treated. For all that, your son will thank you (especially on those hormone-laden days when he's not quite sure what his new bride really wants). Your daughter-in-law will thank you, because she's captured quite the prize: your son.

But then, you knew that all along, didn't you? After all, he's your boy, and you've been planning his wedding for years.

Go ahead—pat yourself on the back. You deserve it.

— 3 —

What Kind of Parent Are You?

What influenced you to become the parent you
are? What's your parenting style—and how does
that affect Little or Big Fletcher?

I f you had to confess, which of these statements sound
familiar?

- "I *told* you to do it."
- "Oh, don't worry about it. Mommy can do it for you."
- "Are you sure you're done with your homework?"
- "I don't care what you think about dinner. Just eat it!"
- "Go back to bed now. I put you in bed once; I'm not
  putting you there again—and no, you can't have a drink
  of water!"
- "Of course, I'll make sure you have that special shirt for
  tomorrow."

- "I told you that you couldn't have that. . . . Well, all right . . . just this once."

Now let me ask you: Do any of those statements that have come out of your mouth sound like ones that came out of your mom's or dad's mouth?

Ah, now you're getting it. You see, as much as you tell yourself, *I'm never going to say to my kids what my mom and dad said to me*, you *will* end up saying it—and you'll say it even with the same tone and expression that your parents used on you! You can inoculate your son from certain diseases, but you'll always pass your own parents' influence on to your kids. Sometimes that's good; other times it can be toxic.

And here's the kicker. As we've already discussed, the opposite-sex relationships are the most important. Since you're a girl, that means your most important relationship was with your father. What kind of dad did you have? Was he:

- a continual, loving presence in your home? Someone who wouldn't miss a game or a band concert or a ballet recital of yours?
- a workaholic who was rarely home for dinner—or for any family activity?
- a stern man who punished you severely for the slightest infraction?
- an alcoholic who embarrassed you in front of your friends?
- a total pushover who would give you anything you wanted?
- a mousy man who was controlled by his wife—your mother?

To Think About

- How did your dad treat you? Do you have any unresolved issues as a result?
- Are there ways in which your son reminds you of your father, or of things that annoy you about your husband, your ex, or the man who fathered your son? In what way do these feelings influence the way you treat your son?
- How did your mom treat you? Was it similar to how your dad treated you, or the exact opposite? How did her treatment make you feel? Do you have any unresolved issues as a result?
- Use a two-column list in a journal (or talk with a trusted friend) to help you separate your feelings about your father from your feelings about your son.

Your relationship with your dad has everything to do with the way you think of and treat your husband (if you're married), men in general, and your son in particular. Any frustrations you experienced with your dad can be passed on to your son through you just because your son is a male. Is your son your dad? No, but you can unconsciously view him that way.

And let's not leave your mom out of the picture. Was your mom:

- a calm-in-crisis, loving presence in your home?
- a smother mother, even if she said it was for your own good?
- so overprotective she embarrassed you in front of your friends?
- flaw-picking and fault-finding?
- balanced in her expectations of you in various stages?
- a total pushover woman you could control?
- so critical you could never do anything right?

- controlling?
- someone who gave you anything you wanted, when you wanted it?

Did your mom treat you the same way Dad did? Or were you caught in the middle of a yo-yo effect, where one parent treated you one way and the other treated you the opposite? For example, was Mom hard on you but you were the apple of Daddy's eye? Or was your father cold and unapproachable while your mom lavished love on you? Did you often feel like you were caught in the middle, not quite sure what to do? If you did one thing, you'd please one parent and make the other one angry. So sometimes you chose not to do anything at all, and you got in trouble for that too.

Who you are today—as an individual and as a parent—has everything to do with the way your mom and dad parented you. And that parenting style will continue to be your gut reaction—your way of doing things. That doesn't mean you can't change, though, if you want to. You have adopted that parenting style by default, because it's what was role modeled to you. So are you going to stay with what's comfortable? Or are you determined to be the best parent you can be for the sake of your son?

It all starts with understanding your parenting style and how it influences you and your son. There are three types of parents. Which style most fits you?

"I'm in Charge, and You Better Believe It! Now Hop to It!"

An *authoritarian parent* barks out an order and expects her son to obey. And it's always done in the tone that holds an

Authoritarian Parents:

- see their child as "little," and themselves as bigger and better.
- allow no freedom for individuality in their child or for anything to happen beyond their control.
- make all decisions for the child.
- use reward and punishment to control their child.

inherent warning: "Do it or I'll . . ." With authoritarian parents, there's no room to be wrong. They are always right, and they expect their children to obey exactly when they tell them to, no questions asked. And if the son doesn't do what Mom says? He's in big trouble. Life is played out on Mom's terms. She's the queen bee, and her worker-bee son doesn't get any say. There's no freedom for him. It's Mom's way or the highway.

If this is you, where do you think you got that style of parenting from? Hands down, my guess is that it came from one or both of your parents as you grew up. At the root of authoritarianism is the belief, "I'm bigger than you. I'm better than you. So you have to do what I tell you to do—or else." In authoritarian homes, children don't have a lot of say. They're merely told to keep quiet and do what they're told. Does that sound like life for you growing up?

On the surface, the authoritarian style of parenting may seem to work. After all, children are mostly too scared of the consequences to open their mouths. The home runs "smoothly" due to the very distinct pecking order. There's usually the king rooster, the mama hen (who runs around doing the bidding of the king rooster), and a bunch of little chicks who don't know what to do or where to go until they're given orders. But what does such a pecking order say to children? That men are most important, then women, and then children.

65

Many times, those who grow up in an authoritarian home also grow up in a conservatively religious home. But let me ask you: is God authoritarian? It says in the Bible that parents are to be *in authority* over their children: "Children, obey your parents; this is the right thing to do because God has placed them in authority over you."[1] But does that verse say parents are supposed to order their children around as if they're automatons and not children loved by God and given to those parents? Does God go around flexing his muscles and pushing his weight around, demanding that we kowtow to him? Or does he wait gently, prompting our hearts to know and understand him better? God almighty doesn't say, "Accept me into your heart—or else." Because he loves his creations—us—he gives us the choice to love him back. After all, forced love and obedience isn't really love or obedience after all, is it? There's no will involved.

> *Authoritarian parents say, "I know what's best for my child, so I make the decisions."*

That's what the authoritarian style of parenting does. It takes all decisions away from the child so that he couldn't possibly make a mistake. How could he? He's never allowed to decide. Authoritarian parents say, "I know what's best for my child, so I make the decisions."

The problem is, that son is never given a chance to fly on his own or to fail. He is simply controlled by fear of punishment if he doesn't do what the parent says, or he's rewarded if he follows the parent's specific wishes.

If you bring your son up with the authoritarian style, you'll create a powerful child who will rebel against the family standards as soon as he gets out from under your thumb. Chances are good he'll choose the lifestyle *opposite* of the

What This Mom Did Right

We moved to a new town when my son, Andrew, was eight. He had a hard time fitting in. He's not really a risk taker. I guess I'm not either. After my husband left when Andrew was four, we've both kinda kept to ourselves. But I could tell Andrew was lonely. All the other boys had known each other since kindergarten. We talked about how Andrew could break the ice with the other boys, but it just didn't happen.

One day in November, it hit me. If I couldn't step out of my own loneliness and make friends, how could I expect Andrew to?

So Andrew and I planned a little party. We invited all eight boys from his class over. It was awkward at first, but then, when we started the games, the boys had a great time.

The next day, when I picked up Andrew from school, he was walking up the sidewalk with two other boys. They were dueling with sticks.

Sometimes taking a risk pays off. But I learned that in order to help my son, I had to risk a little myself too.

Angelica, Texas

one he's grown up with, since living with you was no picnic. Worse, since he's not used to making any decisions for himself, he's not likely to make good decisions. And because he hasn't been allowed any freedom, any individuality, he'll have little self-worth. Since he didn't have any say in his own family growing up, he's not likely to create healthy family dynamics on his own—not without a lot of help from almighty God.

"Oh, Sure, Honey, Whatever You Want to Do Is Just Fine."

Permissive parents are the flip side of authoritarian parents. Instead of controlling their children, their children control them. This is the parent who says, "Oh, Barney,

Permissive Parents:

- believe and act like their child is the center of the universe.
- rob their child of self-respect by doing things for him that he should do for himself.
- are inconsistent yo-yos, based on their child's demands.
- make their child's life Easy Street.

could you turn down that music in there? I'm trying to do your homework, and this science project is due tomorrow!" These parents are so hung up on the child winning in life and—oh my goodness—*never* failing that they literally disable the child by doing things the child should do for himself.

If you want disaster and chaos in your life, do *everything* for your son. Remind your 12-year-old to bring gym clothes on the days he has gym class, and you set him up to be the high schooler who doesn't study for his math test because he didn't learn to write things down, as well as the architect who forgets that a key project is due the next day.

Don't rob your son of the ability to stand on his own two feet both now and in the future. Learning to be responsible and accountable for your actions are two qualities that are vital to life as a well-balanced adult.

Parents who tell their children, "Oh, whatever you want to do is okay," are trying too hard to be their child's friends. But they're not the child's friends; they're the *parents*. And parents are on this earth to be in healthy authority over their children. In other words, they need to be the ones steering the family boat, not letting it flounder all over the ocean until it hits some rocks on shore and sinks.

Are you trying too hard to be your child's friend?

"But I really want my son to like me," one mom told me after I spoke at a church in Ohio. "I just don't want to be hard on him."

I had that woman pegged from her first few words . . . and from the way she was wringing the bottom of her sweater.

"Tell you the truth," I told her, "if you want to be your child's friend, you'll end up being exactly the opposite. If you need a friend, sign up for a mothers' group. But don't expect your three-year-old to meet your friendship requirements. It's just not possible, and it's not smart."

Kids are funny creatures—and I mean that in both definitions of the word. They don't always do or want what you think. However, in all my years of counseling, I've seen that children who grow up in permissive environments rebel.

"I don't get it," you're saying if you're a permissive parent. "Why would they rebel? I give them everything they could ever want."

No, you're missing something. Children need guidelines and limits in order to feel safe at home and to feel comfortable. They need order in their lives. When anything goes and the rules are continually changing, your son won't feel safe. In fact, he'll feel angry because everything about his world constantly changes.

Letting your son do anything at any time and giving him everything he wants isn't love. You're actually teaching your son to be a taker rather than a giver. You're teaching him that the world is all about him, and that no one else matters. Now is that the child you want to raise and send out into the world?

Have you ever seen the movie *Willy Wonka & the Chocolate Factory*, in which selected children won a "golden ticket" to get to visit the famous chocolate factory? Here's the poignant part: every single child in that movie was a "gimme, gimme,

---

Quick Quiz

Read the following statements taken from the beginning of this chapter. Which would be said by an authoritarian parent? Which would be said by a permissive parent?

- "I *told* you to do it."
- "Oh, don't worry about it. Mommy can do it for you."
- "Are you sure you're done with your homework?"
- "I don't care what you think about dinner. Just eat it!"
- "Go back to bed now. I put you in bed once; I'm not putting you there again—and no, you can't have a drink of water!"
- "Of course, I'll make sure you have that special shirt for tomorrow."
- "I told you that you couldn't have that. . . . Well, all right . . . just this once."

See answers on pages 251–52.[2]

---

it's all about me" child—and raised to be that way—except for the very poor Charlie, who was astounded at the way the others acted.

Children who are the products of permissive parents won't learn the value of give-and-take in a healthy relationship. They're too focused on themselves.

The Better Way

Authoritarian and permissive parenting styles are both extremes, but there's a far better way to parent. It's called *authoritative* parenting. Authoritative parents are in healthy authority over their kids. They don't grab them by the scruff of the neck and micromanage them. They don't leave them floundering either. Authoritative parents believe that you can't have love without discipline. Saint Paul said it best, so let me quote that verse again: "Children, obey your parents; this is the right thing to do because God has placed them in authority over you."[3]

Authoritative parents are loving and consistent in their discipline. The child knows exactly what to expect. When Mama says no, she means no, and she's not going to be swayed for any reason. No yo-yo there.

She also gives her child age-appropriate choices. For example, she asks her 5-year-old, "Would you like to have peanut butter and jelly sandwiches for lunch, or macaroni and cheese?" She might tell her 14-year-old, "Sure, we can have a birthday party. If you want to eat out at that place you mentioned and go bowling afterward, you can pick three friends to join us. If you want me to make lasagna and cake and have it at our house, and maybe watch a movie, we could have 10 or 15 friends join you for the party. Just let me know which you prefer." Mom is still setting the boundaries but giving the child the ability to choose. That gives the child credit for having a brain and for being able to make a decision. And that leads to true self-worth.

Oftentimes the rules that kids set for themselves are more stringent than the ones you'd suggest.

Mom not only sets guidelines for the way the home will be run but also has a family meeting so every member of the family gets a say. And here's the interesting thing: oftentimes the rules that kids set for themselves are more stringent than the ones you'd suggest.

Take Frank, for instance, who has had his license for two years. When his mom asked him what he thought the guidelines should be for his curfew and who could be in the car, she was thinking, *I'd like to make sure you're home by 10:00. If you're not, then I want you to call me. And you shouldn't have any more than three friends with you in the car.*

71

When she and Frank met about the guidelines, Frank had his own suggestions. "Mom, I think I should be home by 9:30. If I'm not, I'll give you a call. Would it be okay if I got a cell phone, if I paid for the phone and all the charges with the money I make at the T-shirt shop? And I promise, no more than two friends in the car with me at any time. How does that sound?"

His smart mom nodded as if his ideas were wonderful (and they were), then couldn't help the grin that sprang to her face when she turned and went into the kitchen.

Authoritative parents love their children—but they also hold them accountable for their actions. They use something I call "reality discipline"—a term I coined in 1984—to train and correct their kids. Basically, it means, "Let nature take its course." This means that if your child chooses to do something, then he should bear the consequences for that action. After all, isn't that the way the world works?

So if your son gets a new bike for his birthday and leaves it out in the rain and it rusts, what do you do?

The authoritarian parent would browbeat the kid. "You are such an idiot! Why didn't you pick your bike up? What, you think money grows on trees? Well, I'm not going to get you another bike, ever—and that's final!"

The permissive parent says, "Oh, honey, that's too bad. We'll have to go to the store tonight. Would you rather have the bike in a different color this time?"

The authoritative parent waits until the child notices that the bike's bolts have rusted from being outside and brings it into the garage. When the boy is upset about his new toy being damaged, the authoritative parent says, "I guess that's what happens when it gets left out in the rain, huh? You might be able to loosen those bolts if you use some WD-40. It's in the garage on the second shelf down."

Authoritative Parents:

- are loving and consistent in their discipline.
- present age-appropriate choices.
- let every family member have their say.
- hold their child accountable for his actions.
- let reality be the teacher.

What has the authoritative parent done? She's put the bike back in the child's court. Who left the bike out in the rain? The boy did. So who should have to suffer the consequences to fix it? The boy ought to do the work! Now, if the boy has worked for four hours on the bike and still not gotten anywhere, the authoritative parent might poke her head out into the garage and say, "How's it going out here? Need any help?"

Adopting such a parenting style doesn't mean you don't help your son when he needs it, but that you make him responsible and hold him accountable for his own actions. His bike may not look new anymore, and it may have some rusty bolts your son will have to struggle with for the lifetime of the bike. But do you think your son learned a lesson that will stick with him? You bet!

What Kind of Parent Are You?

Which of the three types of parents in this chapter—authoritarian, permissive, or authoritative—sounded most like you?

If you're an authoritarian parent, you need to back off and give your child some freedom, even if it's freedom to fail. Smothering or over-mothering your son will only make him rebel against you and everything you believe and stand for down the road. And it won't prepare your son well for life.

If you're a permissive parent, stand up for yourself. Not later but right now. Who's the parent anyway? You or your child? Stop trying to be your child's friend, and *be the parent*. Your son probably won't like it at first—after all, he's used to the old you he can push around. But not anymore. Decide that today is the day things will change in the house—for your own peace of mind and for your son's sake.

If you're an authoritative parent, you've already heaped blessings on your son both now and for the future. Good for you! You're doing great. However, keep your eyes on your goal. Your greatest challenge will be in sticking to your parenting style as your son moves through all the phases of his life, particularly those adolescent years, where you might not think you figure quite so high on your son's totem pole anymore.

Sticking to It

Here comes the rub. You know what kind of parent you are, why you are that way, and what you need to do to balance your parenting style toward the healthy authoritative style. You're determined to do something about it, so you forge ahead. "But, Dr. Leman"—you sigh—"there are simply *those days*." Your eye roll (reminiscent of the one you got from your son exactly 16 times today) says it all.

Yes, Mom, there are those days. The days when you're not at your best, and you're a little too worn down to act on the principles you're determined to follow. But don't get down on yourself and call yourself a failure. Each day is a new day and a new chance to follow that commitment.

Here are a few hints to help you along the way.

Don't Just Use Words—Act

Your kids are no dummies. As soon as you open your mouth, they've got you pegged. They know what you're going to say . . . and say . . . and say . . . No wonder they tune you out. Since you as a woman are wired to be verbal, it's hard to keep your mouth shut. But you'll find that if you say less, you'll actually accomplish a lot more.

You see, it's *words* that get you into trouble. If you're an authoritarian parent, you've threatened so much that when your kids see you coming, they simply duck out or get busy doing something else you've asked them to do that they haven't done yet. If you're a permissive parent, they already know that if they push hard enough, you'll say, "Well, that's okay for this time,

> *If your words are getting you in trouble, try something simple. Close your mouth.*

but no more." What are your words really saying? "Okay, kids, it's a free-for-all. Come and get it. And if you do it to me again next time, you'll also get off."

So if your words are getting you in trouble, try something simple. Close your mouth. Ask your child once (kindly, straightforwardly) to do what you'd like him to do. Then don't mention it again. If your son doesn't do what you ask, have someone else do that task for him.

Cary, a permissive parent, had allowed her son, Josh, to get a guinea pig. Why she'd been talked into it, she never could figure out—until she heard me talk about permissive parents on a nationwide radio show. Then the lightbulb went on.

"I didn't want the poor critter to starve," Cary said, "but I was sick of feeding the guinea pig and cleaning his cage. It was just another job I had to do, and it was *his* pet. So one Wednesday, I told him that he needed to be responsible to feed his own guinea pig. I just got the wave and a 'Yeah, Mom.' I closed my mouth and didn't say anything else. On Thursday, Friday, and Saturday, I fed the guinea pig.

"Then the big moment came on Sunday, when Josh usually got his allowance. I had deducted three dollars for every time I fed his pet and five dollars for the time I had to clean the cage. When Josh got his allowance envelope, he ran off with it to his room, as usual. But a couple minutes later, he came back, looking puzzled. 'Uh, Mom,' he said, 'I don't think you counted right. There're 14 dollars missing.' It was the perfect teachable moment, I tell you." She laughed when she told me about it. "It's been a month since then, and Josh has only forgotten to feed that guinea pig once."

Actions work. Enough said.

Be a Role Model for Your Own Values

Your son can sense a phony from a mile away. If you tell him he always has to be honest, and then you tell a "little white lie" to a colleague when you don't want to attend a dinner, he'll catch on. If you tell your son he should never cheat, and then he overhears you and your husband talking about not including that little 500 bucks from a freelance project on your income-tax form, what message are you sending your son?

Values are caught rather than taught.

Values are caught rather than taught. And what you do speaks much louder to your son than what you say.

But here's the good news: if your child can catch you when you make mistakes, he can also catch you doing good. If he hears you talking on the phone to a friend who has just lost her job and is very discouraged, then sees you packing up the homemade chicken soup and leftover rolls from tonight's

What You Can Do

- Brainstorm what steps you need to take to be the parent you want to be.
- Stick to "the plan."
- Remember, it's all about connecting with your child. And nobody else can take your place.

dinner and putting them in the car to bring to her, what does that say to your son? *Hey, Mom helps other people.* And it translates to his mind as, *Hmm, I wonder how I could help someone?*

Remember, Mom, it all goes back to that little secret I shared at the beginning of the book. Your boy wants to please you. He wants your approval. So what better thing to share with him to emulate than the values that you hold dear and want him to carry with him the rest of his life? That's what will stick with your boy, because he's watching you far more than you know.

Make It All about the Relationship

At the end of the day, parenting is not about rules. It's about the relationship—the connection between you and your son. The rules are secondary. After all, as I stated earlier, if there is no relationship, no rules will work because your son won't care about following them.

Your son will break a lot of rules as he's growing up. Some you'll know about, others you won't (until much later, when the stories are shared belatedly at a family dinner, and you're both older and wiser). Parenting is not about sticking to the rules like glue. It's not about flaw-picking everything your child does. It's not about giving kids what they want just to keep them happy and out of your hair or to make them "feel good" about themselves. It's about teaching your children to be givers, not takers, to think of others rather than just themselves. It's about developing a sense of love, loyalty, integrity, and support that extends beyond your immediate home to your son's future home with his own wife and children, and into the world that he touches.

Sure, you'll make mistakes. Every parent does. But if you keep your focus on maintaining a relationship with your son through all his ages and stages, you'll never go wrong.

4

Understanding Fletcher

Why is Fletcher the way he is? Why do he and his siblings squabble? Here are the secrets to knowing when to step in and when to butt out and let them handle it.

I just don't understand it. I've got two boys, and they're both so different," one mom told me. "One does everything I ask him. And the other? He goes out of his way to do things differently, or not at all. He even talks his brother into doing his jobs around the house sometimes. I don't know how, but he does. I don't get it. I'm raising both boys the same way, and they live in the same house. So why do they act the opposite?"

"Ah. You've hit the nail on the head, Mom," I told her, smiling. "Just because you've got two birds in your cozy little nest doesn't mean they'll act anything like each other. In fact, they're most likely to be polar opposites.

"Let me go further and make some guesses. Your one son who does everything you ask him is your firstborn son. He's responsible, he's organized, he works hard, and he's a bit of a perfectionist. When he was younger, little things bothered him, like the tag in the back of his shirt or the wrinkle in his sock. He just wants to see the job done and done right, so no wonder he picks up the slack from his brother sometimes.

"And your other son? He's the baby of the family. The charmer who gets away with murder. He's really good at getting others—especially his older brother—to do things he doesn't want to do. He just acts helpless or procrastinates, and his brother gives up and does it for him. He's good at making people laugh, and people probably think he's cute."

The mom stared at me, wide-eyed. "How could you *know* all that? You pegged them perfectly!"

All Your Little Birds in the Family Nest

It's easy to think that just because you have two or more birds in the family nest, they'll all act the same. After all, they live in the same house, follow the same rules, and probably follow a similar schedule (unless they are spread far apart in age). If you birthed them and they have the same father, they even share genes. So of course they'd be the same. Right?

Wrong! Just living with those birds assures you that they're very different, doesn't it? That's because each of your fledglings has a different place on the family tree. In fact, one of the best predictions in life is that whatever the firstborn in a family is and does, the secondborn in the family will go in a different (and oftentimes opposite) direction. And as much as you try to make your relationship with your children "equal and the same," there will always be one who is your favorite and one you always want to knock off his perch because the two of you clash so much.

The more you understand who your son is, the easier it'll be to relate to him as he grows. You'll be able to figure out what he's thinking and why he does what he does.

But before we go any further, stop and take this Quick Quiz.

Quick Quiz

Which description sounds *most* like your son? (If you have more than one son, take this quiz for each of them.)

- He goes out of his way to avoid conflicts. He's the mediator and very diplomatic. He is loyal to his many friends and compromises so that others will like him. He's independent, a maverick, and secretive. He's not used to having attention at home, so he finds it elsewhere—in his peers.
- You can always count on him. He is a natural leader, takes life seriously (including his studies), is a perfectionist, and is well organized. He loves to read. He's conscientious, critical, logical, technically oriented, and a list maker. He drives himself (and others) and doesn't like surprises.
- He's a charmer, an attention seeker, and a people person. He could sell ice to Eskimos. He is engaging, is affectionate, and loves surprises. The world revolves around him. He blames others when something goes wrong (it's never his fault). He often gets away with murder because he's cute.
- He is a little adult and feels more comfortable with people who are older or younger. He's self-motivated, a voracious reader, and a high achiever. He thinks in black and white—no grays allowed—and talks in extremes ("always," "never"). He's very thorough in everything he does and expects a lot out of himself. He is cautious and can't stand the idea of failing at any task.

See answers on page 252.[1]

What Place Does Your Son Have on the Family Tree?

Where does your son fit in the lineup on the family tree? Was he born or adopted first? Second? Last? His birth order in the family has everything to do with who your son is, why he is the way he is, and who he will become. That's because the order in which your children were born has a lot to do with how they learn and perceive reality. And that's why, years later at a family reunion, your firstborn might remember the same family event a lot differently than your baby of the family. Each birth order perceives the family differently.

Is birth order an exact science? No, because not all characteristics fit every person in that birth order, and there are also variables that can change your child's birth order (we'll talk briefly about those later). But I've been around the block enough times—and seen how birth order principles work for thousands and thousands of families—to be a staunch believer in birth order. So do me a favor: if you think the whole idea of birth order is a bunch of hogwash, just give me this chapter to change your mind. You'll not only understand your son, you'll understand yourself a whole lot better too.

Your Firstborn

Since your oldest is born first, he has an advantage that no other child in the family has. He's got Mom and Dad (if a two-parent family) or you, Mom, all to himself for a while! So it's no surprise that he tends to act more like a little adult. After all, he's had only his parent(s) for role models.

The firstborn is your guinea pig. You're just figuring out parenting, and he's your science experiment. When he picks up dog plop and tries to eat it because the texture looks interesting, you're horrified, and you make sure you wash his hands 13 times and wash his mouth out 5 times just in case the foul substance actually entered any orifice. (By the third child, you're saying, "Oh, that? Well, it won't hurt him. After all, it's natural.") Everything he does wrong is heightened, and you tend to react more quickly and with a more excited tone. "Don't touch that!" you'll say when he reaches for a plant. (By the time you get to that third child, the poor plant is tattered and you've forgotten to water it, so what does it matter?)

Firstborns are often achievers. They tend to walk and talk and have a larger vocabulary at a younger age. After all, they're spending their time interacting with an adult who's got a bigger vocabulary rather than a brother who just grunts.

Firstborns are perfectionistic. New situations tend to make them nervous because they don't like making mistakes or failing.

Firstborns are perfectionistic. New situations tend to make them nervous because they don't like making mistakes or failing. They're less likely to answer questions in class because they might be wrong. They come by this caution naturally, since their new-to-parenting parents always reacted strongly to anything they did and have higher expectations for their firstborn than for any other birth order. (With the birth or adoption of each child, the superhuman expectations of Mom and Dad are shaved down more to reality.)

Your firstborn will also have a keen sense of right and wrong. He'll insist that there's a "right way" to do things, and in his mind, anything else is "wrong." That's why it drives him crazy when his younger siblings do certain tasks. A famous statement of a firstborn is, "Here, let me help you with that." Then he proceeds to undo what the other person did so he can do it "better."

He'll be reliable and conscientious, and he'll enjoy making lists to organize himself.

He's also a leader—the one his peers turn to—and very achievement oriented. Getting As on his report card is extremely important to him.

Your Only Child

If you have only one child, it's most likely he's a firstborn on steroids. That means he'll take on all the characteristics of the firstborn child times three. Books are an only child's best friends; they become like siblings and companions.

Only children act mature way beyond their years—they are little adults by age seven or eight. They work independently. And they can't understand why kids in other families fight.

Your Middleborn

Middleborns are indeed in the middle. They're not the super-achieving, superhuman firstborn, and they're not the cute baby of the family either. That means they live in the middle—in a rather hazy, anonymous world where they are often not noticed. That means they can get away with occasional laziness because the spotlight isn't on them. For that reason, they aren't pushed quite as hard or expected to accomplish quite as much as their firstborn sibling.

Whatever your middleborn child is or does will be the opposite of the child above him in the family. If your firstborn plays by all the rules and is very traditional, the second will be and do the exact opposite. *After all*, he thinks, *how on earth can I compete with my big brother? Why bother? I'll just do something else.*

84

Firstborns are focused on achievement and pushing themselves. Middleborns are very loyal and big on friendships. That's why you'll often find them in a cluster of friends.

Oftentimes your middleborn will be the peacemaker of the family—stuck between your hard-driving firstborn and your can't-get-it-all-together-or-get-anything-done baby of the family. Your middleborn just wants everyone to get along so the waters of life will stay smooth.

> *Your middleborn just wants everyone to get along so the waters of life will stay smooth.*

Your Lastborn

He's your funny one. Your social one. Your manipulative charmer. There's nothing he can't get his siblings (or anyone else) to do for him if he tries hard enough. After all, he's the littlest one in the family, so just how *could* he do that chore anyway? He's social and outgoing, and he makes people laugh. Babies of the family often become the class clowns—entertaining, but they can drive the teacher crazy.

Your lastborn is your child most likely to walk up to a stranger and engage him in conversation. He's never met a person he can't talk to.

To a baby of the family, life is a thrill ride because it's all about being spontaneous. He has a great sense of humor and is the family entertainer.

He's also the one most likely to get away with murder and least likely to be punished. The problem is, his siblings know it, so he's the one they send on missions to check out what you're doing when you've already put the kids to bed—twice.

Do you recognize some of your son's traits in these birth orders? How about some of your own?

If you're saying, "Well, my son is a firstborn, but he doesn't have any of those traits," or "my middleborn acts like a firstborn" here's why.

If Your Son Doesn't Fit the Mold

Birth order is a description of tendencies, not a black-and-white checklist. It isn't just about your number in the family. If it were, I wouldn't have needed to write a whole book about it.[2] Birth order is also affected by a variety of variables—different factors or forces that have an impact on each person.

Spacing

The number of years between children is a crucial variable. If there is a gap of more than five or six years between children, the next child born actually starts a new "family." That next-born child may have all the characteristics of a firstborn even though he's the lastborn. But because he's the littlest and is treated as such by others in the family, he may also have some baby-of-the-family characteristics.

The Sex of Each Child

If your firstborn child is a female and your secondborn child is a male, that secondborn child will most likely act like a firstborn. Why? Because he's the firstborn *male* in the family. Since the firstborn child is a girl, there isn't as much competition for the secondborn, so he doesn't have to go in the opposite direction to be noticed. However, if his firstborn sister is too perfect, the secondborn male who acts like a firstborn could still have a rebellious streak that may not show itself until later in his teenage years or when he's out of your home.

Physical, Emotional, or Mental Differences

Let's say that your firstborn son is smaller than average. Then your secondborn son arrives. Already at birth, he's got your firstborn outweighed by five pounds, and he continues to grow. It doesn't take a genius to see how people will think of the secondborn as the firstborn and will treat him that way. As a result, the roles of the two boys will be reversed. The same kind of role reversal happens when the firstborn has emotional or mental challenges such as ADHD or Down syndrome.

Adoption

If a child is adopted as an infant, his birth order is set by the family he is adopted into. However, if a child is adopted after the age of three, his birth order has already been set by whatever "family" he had before his adoption, whether that was his birth family, his foster family, or a welfare institution. That means if he's acting as a firstborn and you bring him home to be a sibling to your firstborn five-year-old, a little World War III of competition may erupt right there in your own living room. Understanding where your adopted child came from and the role he played before he came to your home can make all the difference to ease the transition for every family member.

Sibling Death

If an older sibling dies early in life, the child below may be bumped up to the next birth order by default. In the case of young children, that birth order change can happen easily and naturally. But if your son is older—say, 14—and his 16-year-old brother dies in a car crash, then the 14-year-old will become your acting firstborn. However, because he has baby-of-the-family traits, acting as the responsible, driving firstborn will exact a heavy toll on your son.

The Blending of Two Families Because of Death or Divorce

When two families come together, there's a great possibility for a clash. Each individual family has had its own family structure of firstborn, middleborn, and lastborn. When the two families join, no child wants to give up his place in the family. And who can blame him? When families join, the best of all worlds is if one family has younger children (for example, ages 3, 5, and 7) and the other family has older children (for example, ages 13, 15, and 17). If the children overlap in age, there is much greater potential for one child to be dethroned from his position.

> *The biggest thing to remember about birth order is that we are affected and influenced the most by whoever is directly above us in the family.*

The biggest thing to remember about birth order is that we are affected and influenced the most by whoever is directly above us in the family.

What You've Got to Do with It

By now you know what birth order your son is and what variables impact his birth order. But there's an even bigger birth order variable—you.

Your Birth Order

What birth order are you, Mom? What variables affected you in your growing-up years that also affected your birth order? Here's why it's important to know: parents tend to overidentify with the child of the same birth order, and that can lead to too much pressure on that child or too much favoritism toward them. What you expect out of your children and how you treat them is what they will become.

What you expect out of your children and how you treat them is what they will become.

Let's say your two kids are in a big fight, throwing words back and forth. You don't know who did what, and there's no way of being sure of the facts. But you're a firstborn. You remember being told, as you were growing up, "Well, you know better than that. You should have stopped your brother from doing that. After all, he's younger." And you remember how angry that made you feel because what happened wasn't your fault. With those memories in the back of your mind, how do you think you'll react to this tussle between your children?

That firstborn is going to get off the hook, and the secondborn is going to get hammered, whether he did anything or not.

If you're a middleborn, what are you likely to say? "Come on, kids. Can't you just get along?"

If you're a lastborn, you're likely to hold the firstborn accountable. After all, he *is* older and should have known better. And your baby? He's just so cute that he couldn't have done anything wrong.

See how it works?

The more you understand about your own birth order, the more you'll be able to provide balanced parenting for your children.

Your Personality Style

Are you a go-with-the-flow, relaxed type of person or a schedule keeper? Perhaps you're somewhere in between. Your personality style has everything to do with how you relate to your children.

Let's say your children are late coming out of school—not just a little late, but 15 minutes late. What would you do?

- Sit in your car and worry. *Did someone snatch them? Should I be calling the police?*
- Fume, thinking, *Those kids. They're always late. And I've got a schedule to keep. Tonight alone I've got to do . . .*
- Figure, *Well, they must be doing something after school. If they were in trouble, somebody would call me.*
- Drink coffee, turn up the radio, and enjoy some quiet time.

Your answer to that question says a lot about your personality style and how you relate to your kids. Those who are more relaxed will tend to create more relaxed, fun-loving children. Those who pack five after-school activities into the week year after year will tend to create children who don't know how to relax and create their own fun. They feel lost if they're not going somewhere.

If you're a parent who likes to indulge your children, buying them every item their little heart desires, you'll create children who think the world is "all about me." And "when

I want something, I just ask for it and I get it." But does that happen in the real world? Don't set up expectations for your children that aren't grounded in reality, or you'll set them up for disappointment when they're out on their own. There's nothing wrong with a little indulgence every once in a while, but when it becomes a habit, that's a problem.

If you're a parent who tends to be hard on your children, always telling them what they're doing wrong or what they could do better, think of it this way. Would you want someone to constantly tell you what you're doing wrong or what you could do better in your job? How would that come across to you? You would probably feel like, *Boy, I must really be blowing it. He never says anything nice, just harps on what I do wrong.*

How do you think your son feels? As if he can never measure up to your high expectations?

Firstborn moms in particular fall prey to fault-finding. After all, they're black-and-white thinkers. Something can *only* be done one way, and if it's done differently, it's wrong. So firstborns can be tremendous flaw-pickers. Woe to the child who has two firstborn parents, because he'll be nitpicked to death. And if that son is a firstborn, it's even worse. Mom and Dad always have their eye on the firstborn since he's the first to do anything, so he sets the standard. And with a firstborn mom and dad, that standard has to be exceptionally high, in their opinion. Their firstborn gets the brunt of their critical energies, the middleborn is smart enough to escape to his room or blend in with the woodwork, and the baby gets less critical attention since he's little, cute, and seen as less capable, so he isn't held to as high a standard.

The way you view and treat each child is different (even if you think you're treating them equally), so no wonder siblings squabble sometimes.

It Is a Wonderful Life!

In the classic Christmas movie *It's a Wonderful Life*, young George Bailey and his brother, Harry, are roughhousing upstairs in their home. They're making an awful racket, and their parents tell them to quiet down.

The housekeeper, Annie, just shakes her head and says, "You know, all children should be girls."

Why Siblings Squabble

"Mom, he's not taking turns!"

"She started it!"

"Why does *he* always get to stay up so late?"

"You never believe me. He's always right."

Sibling squabbles go way back to the beginning, when the third and fourth people on earth just happened to be siblings. Cain and Abel were as different as night and day, and they certainly didn't get along. Their parents' favoritism most likely had a lot to do with the sad result of Cain's anger.

It's a fact of life: siblings will squabble. No two people living under the same roof will always get along. But how you respond to squabbles has everything to do with whether they end quickly and the children are reconciled, or the squabbles fester and grow into an all-out war.

As the old saying goes, "It takes two to tango," and with any fight, there are two people involved. That means both are responsible for fighting. There's no "Well, you started it" followed by "No, *you* did." One most likely started it, but the other one jumped right on the bandwagon, kicked up the fight, and let it continue. All it takes is a hand gesture, an expression, or a word, and siblings go at it.

By the way, Mom, there's nothing more emotionally satisfying for a boy who is driven to compete than squaring off with his brother and knocking the living daylights out of him. Fighting with a sister doesn't provide the same satisfaction, because girls tend to fight more with words. But in a pinch, a girl will do.

Many parents try to stop sibling fights. "Now come on, guys, kiss and make up."

But the two red-faced bulls aren't about to be done, and cajoling from Mama isn't going to make them finish. They're mad, and both are determined to win. So what can you do?

If your kids want to fight, I say, "Let 'em fight!"

"What?" you're saying. "Are you telling me to let my kids duke it out? They'll kill each other."

Wait. Let me finish. If they want to fight, give them what they want. But *you* have the right to say where the children can fight and under what conditions. They also have to fight fair—no punching, no kicking, no abusive behavior. If the children fight, it cannot interfere with the peace and welfare of others in the home.

When kids start fighting, take them to a room elsewhere in the house. Even better, have them go to the backyard or the deck of your condo, where a neighbor is likely to see them (it's amazing how quickly a fight ends if a third party could be watching).

Tell them, "Okay, so you want to fight. Go right ahead. Keep fighting until you work out your problems. Don't come out until you're done." Then close the door and walk away. (A note for those of you who have children who could be considered bullies or physically aggressive: you might want to stick around within earshot in case you hear any punches landing. If you do, you'd be wise to open that door and step in. But most of the time,

> *If they want to fight, give them what they want.*

your kids will be fighting with words—at least when they've already been called by you on their fighting and moved to another location.)

Here's what's fascinating. When you give your children permission to fight, 99 times out of 100 they won't. They'll merely stand and eye each other, both feeling a little stupid. One might say, "All right, you start it." And the other one replies, "No, *you* start it."

Usually neither of them starts it because they've begun to cool off, and neither wanted to fight that badly. What they really wanted was their parents' attention. Your boys want to involve *you* in their battles. They want *you* to have to take sides. But when you walk away, it deflates the battle. There's really no payoff for the fighting, because it no longer captures your attention.

Then some reality kicks in.

You know, if we fight, I might get hurt.

Little League practice is in an hour. We might miss it.

Huh. It's really not worth it.

The sooner you learn to stay out of your children's tussles, the sooner you'll teach them responsibility, accountability, and how to get along. And you'll be a lot happier too.

Why Treating Everyone Equally Isn't Always the Best Modus Operandi

Let's say that one year for Christmas, you decided that you'd get every child the same present. *After all*, you think, *that would be the fair thing to do.* So you go to your local Sports Authority store and pick up three skateboards to go under the tree. Then you get each of the kids baseball cards for their stockings.

The only problem is, on Christmas morning, only one of your kids is happy—your 8-year-old son who was just dying for the newest skateboard. Your 16-month-old son is looking a little confused, since he just got a handle on walking but can't even walk in a straight line yet, much less skateboard. And your 13-year-old daughter? She's looking downright disgusted. She wanted a Wii, and she got a skateboard?

Every child is unique. So why would you try to treat them all the same?

There's a difference between treating every child with equal love and respect and treating them the same. Every birth order has specific strengths and weaknesses. And that's why you need to parent your children differently.

Secrets to Parenting Your Firstborn

Your firstborn is already driven to do everything and to do it well. He doesn't need you pushing him from behind since he's got enough internal motivation to get the job done. He'll naturally take the lead. But does that mean he should always take the lead or he has to take the lead, even if he's the oldest? Your firstborn has a lot of stresses—he's the first to do anything in the family, so all eyes are on him (yours as well as his siblings'). That's a lot of pressure for a kid to stand up under.

The best thing you can do for your firstborn is lighten up the pressure. Make sure your other children pull their own weight at home. Let your firstborn get special privileges—for example, a bedtime of half an hour or an hour later than his younger siblings (age appropriate, of course). Don't always assume he can be the babysitter or that he should keep track of his younger siblings. Allow him time just to "be"—by himself.

What Does Your Firstborn Need?

- To know his place in the family (and in your heart) is secure.
- That he doesn't have to do everything—or do it right.
- That it's okay to fail.

Also, share with him your failures so that he doesn't think a failure is the end of the world. *Boy, that didn't work out as well as I thought, now did it? Oh well, it's no big deal.*

Ask him what he thinks about things, and give him age-appropriate choices. Remember that he relates the most to adults since he spent time alone with you before his siblings arrived, and he craves that time with you even now but isn't likely to get it without you putting it on your calendar.

Above all, watch your firstborn's schedule so he doesn't get too overloaded. Firstborns tend to take on the world, but sometimes they can take on too much and exhaust themselves or drive themselves crazy.

Secrets to Parenting Your Middleborn

Remember that a middleborn is used to being in the middle, and he can really feel the squeeze. After all, he's stuck between his perfect, driven older sibling and the baby who gets all the attention. Sometimes he wonders how long it would take for someone in the family to notice that he's missing if he went AWOL.

Other times he gets tired of being the peacemaker who's always stuck between the warring parties. He'd rather go off and be with his friends (even if he has to negotiate some battles there too).

For the middleborn, home can be the place where he lives, but he doesn't really feel very important as a member of the family.

> ### What Does Your Middleborn Need?
>
> - To know that he has an important place in the family and that what he thinks and feels matters.
> - To be encouraged in his areas of specific strength.
> - To develop a good core group of friends since they'll be a key part of his life.

The best thing you can do for your middleborn is to show him that he has a special place in the family, and his thoughts, feelings, and opinions matter and you want to hear them. Many middleborns are shyer and more easygoing and are thus unwilling to confront or speak up. So make sure your middleborn is given his say in family activities and meetings.

Help your middleborn make friends. Every time a child makes a friend, he gets practice in committing to relationships and in working at keeping them going. So get to know your middleborn's friends and make opportunities for him to spend time with friends, who are at the center of his world. (Interesting, isn't it, that a middleborn often makes for the happiest and most loyal marriage partner?)

Make sure you give your middle child plenty of opportunities to share with you. Schedule time for a walk or take the child along on an errand when it's just the two of you in the car. By the way, talking in the car is a wonderful option. For a middle child, it feels less confrontational to look out the window and talk than it does to have a sit-down to find out how life is going.

Also, challenge him to do his best and to pursue his interests. Because he's not in the spotlight and isn't pushed as hard as the firstborn, he can tend to sit back and never fulfill his potential. But if you encourage him in his areas of strength, you'll be amazed at what your middleborn can do.

What This Mom Did Right

I have three boys who are 8, 11, and 12. The oldest one and the youngest one get along well. They're always playing baseball or football together. The middle one is always left out. He fights continually with his older brother. They can't seem to get along for more than two minutes without me being in the room. Lately he's started to fight a lot with his younger brother too, who's almost the same height as him now.

I was at my wit's end until a neighbor, seeing the skirmishes, told me, "You know, Deirdre, it sure seems like D.J. is left out a lot when his brothers play. Do you think that bothers him?" I told her I'd tried everything to make his brothers include him in their play, but it never worked and ended in a fight.

"How about having a friend over to play when his brothers have a longer timespan to play together?" she suggested.

A lightbulb went on. I'm not dumb (really, I'm not), but I honestly hadn't thought of that as a solution. I tried it out.

I'm amazed at how well it works. When D.J.'s had time with a friend all to himself, the entire rest of the day with his brothers goes way better. I know it sounds corny, but the change is like a miracle! Our house is so much calmer.

Deirdre, Minnesota

Secrets to Parenting Your Lastborn

He's your little charmer, the little fledgling in the nest who gets the most attention because he's always up to something. He's the entertainer at the family picnic. But beware, Mom. Your baby of the family can really manipulate you! And he's born knowing it. But if you're wise to his setup skills—the way he sets up an older sibling to get in trouble by pestering him relentlessly until the older sibling lashes out and the baby goes running to Mommy for protection—your other kids won't be crying, "Foul!"

Your baby is also born at a time when you're a little worn down as a parent. You're already juggling multiple children, so it's easy to look the other way when he skips doing his chores. Then later you ask an older sibling to do

> ### What Does Your Lastborn Need?
>
> - To know that life isn't a continual party—that he has to pull his own weight in the family. Fun is a good thing, but sometimes you have to get the job done too.
> - To realize that not everyone will think he's cute or that what he does is cute.
> - To learn how to think through situations and see the consequences before he acts.
> - To realize that manipulating others will only go so far . . . before his brothers will pound lumps on him.

that chore. That way you know it'll get done—and done a lot faster.

But is that really what your lastborn needs? Like all children, he needs to learn responsibility and that he will be held accountable for his actions. After all, someday he's going to be a grown-up, right? Will you then go over to his apartment to tie his shoes for him? To do his laundry? I doubt it. Your lastborn needs to step up to the plate and play an active role to help in the family.

Sure, he'll always be your social, outgoing one. But he needs to learn how to juggle his penchant for relationships and fun with a little reality check on what needs to happen for life to run smoothly for everyone in your family.

Understanding Fletcher

When you understand your child's birth order and any variables that have affected it, as well as your own birth order and parenting style, you're way ahead of the game and the majority of parents, who can sometimes be clueless (even if they do have PhDs behind their names). So why not pass the

What You Can Do

- Treat each child as an individual.
- Make time to spend time with each child—just you and him.
- Avoid comparing one child with another.
- Make sure each child pulls his own weight in the family.

word along about birth order? It certainly makes for fascinating conversations around the family dinner table.

And you can smile secretly as you see siblings look at each other with that "Aha, now I know why you act like you do!" expression.

Believe me, that knowledge comes in mighty handy.

5

Discipline That Works—
Every Time

*Say no to those daily battles with your son with
a no-fail plan.*

I won't!"
"You can't make me."
"Nah, nah, nah, nah, I can't hear you!" (said while hold-ing his ears).

For any mom, those are fightin' words. They just trigger the worst in you, don't they? You feel that flush start up your neck, your face gets red, then your ears, and the steam starts to blow out the top of your head. No mom can stand a disrespectful kid for long.

If you're tired of the whining, the complaining, the bicker-ing, the sassy mouth, and the fighting that goes on in your house, isn't it time to try something different?

I've got just the plan, and it really works. In fact, it's been tried with thousands and thousands of families nationwide, and moms who use it are grinning from ear to ear. It's taken the stress right out of their day . . . and the wind right out of their kid's sails.

Getting Off to a Good Start

Some of you are still in the early years of parenting, when it's easy to change the road you're on. Others of you have already reached the adolescent years, when the wet cement of your son has started to harden and changes are more hard-won.

But let me assure you, it's never too late to start, no matter what age or stage your child is. If you want a child who is loving, kind, and self-disciplined—in other words, not like other kids!—make developing such a child a priority.

"What do you mean, Dr. Leman?" you might be saying. "Not like other kids? But I want my son to be like every other boy. If he's different, he'll get picked on."

My goodness! If that's the way you think, I feel sorry for you. Do you really want your son to be just like every other boy?

Take a look around. It won't take long. Check out the screaming toddlers with their cajoling mothers in the grocery store. Watch the kindergartener who yells "No!" at his mother, punches her in the stomach, and runs off. Watch the fourth grader who's already got attitude with a capital A, yet his mother is surfing the net to surprise him with the latest gizmo that costs more than their first mortgage payment. Watch the 16-year-old who

Do you really want your son to be just like every other boy?

lets his mom have it full force for not getting his favorite T-shirt washed for school, then holds out his hands for the car keys.

Now let me ask you, why are these kids acting that way?

The answer is simple: because their parents are letting them get away with it. And the one who usually lets them get away with the most is Mom. Why is that? Usually Mom's the one who's with them 24-7 (or pretty close to it), and frankly, she gets worn down. You know what I mean, because you're probably feeling that way right now as you read this book.

Many of today's kids are out of control, mean-spirited, and disrespectful of both themselves and everyone else. And there's a reason for that.

The "Feeling Good" Trap

I'm convinced, from all the moms I've talked with and counseled, that many mothers are overly concerned with a child's self-esteem.

"But I want Bryan to feel good about himself," one mom told me after I did a seminar on my book *Have a New Kid by Friday*. So what did that mom do? She went on to tell me all the ways she's tried to help Bryan feel good about himself.

When he didn't get up in time for school, she called the school and lied by telling them he had a doctor appointment and was running late, then even drove him to McDonald's for an Egg McMuffin when he didn't want the breakfast she'd made. Another time, he forgot his trumpet for a rehearsal. She left her own workplace to drive home, pick up the trumpet, and bring it to him at school.

But what was she really doing? Snowplowing her son's life for him. That kid lived totally on Easy Street. No wonder he was a behavioral nightmare and she looked completely exhausted!

Who do you think that mother is raising? Not a son. A *tyrant* who will expect things his own way, in his own time, and will run over everyone else. That mother may think she's helping her son with his self-esteem, but what is she really doing? She's sending the message, "Oh, here, Son. Mommy will do it for you. You don't have to be responsible for anything."

Then there's Kara, who always reminds her son, Sean, when it's his night to put the dishes in the dishwasher. You know what he's really hearing by her constant reminders? "You're so stupid that I don't think you'll remember, so I have to say it every time." Do you think that's what she wants to convey? No wonder Sean sometimes gets "mommy deaf." He's got good reason.

> *Doing things your son should do for himself isn't being respectful of him.*

Doing things your son should do for himself isn't being respectful of him. If he forgets something, what should you do? A little reality discipline is in order. If you forgot to go to work one day, do you think somebody would notice you missing and there would be consequences? So why should you snowplow your child's road when your son is too lazy to get up for school? If he's lazy later in life, the stakes are higher. He'll lose his job. Why not let him find out the hard way now, while he's safe in your nest?

There's a big difference between self-esteem and self-worth. They may both sound the same—feeling good about yourself—but the results are far different. Making a child feel good is easy. Just give him everything he wants and do everything for him so he doesn't have to lift a finger. He'll certainly feel

---

The 3 Things That Matter Most in Your Son's Life

- Attitude
- Behavior
- Character

How is your son doing? Is he the kind of person you'd want to hire if you were a potential supervisor someday? If not, what needs to change?

---

good—for a time. But the children who have true self-worth feel good about themselves because *they themselves* have done something.

"Jeremiah, you made the bed. And all by yourself. Oh, that's wonderful!" you could say in response to your three-year-old's first efforts. Just watch that boy puff out his chest and do some swaggering around your living room. That's because he did something himself. And next time he'll make an even bigger effort.

Feeling good is temporary. It's not your job as a parent to make your son feel good about himself. As I often say, "An unhappy child is a healthy child."

Look at it this way. Is your day always happy? Is it perfect? Does everyone do what you ask them to do? Does your workday go perfectly? Or are there a few flaws throughout the day? So why should your child expect an always-perfect day? Trying to smooth your child's road sets up an unrealistic expectation for him about the way life will be. Why not let your son deal with some of the disappointment now? If so, he'll develop a resilient spirit. When things hit him in his adult years, they won't knock him down. He'll get up, dust himself off, and say, "Well, that was interesting. Okay, so what's next?"

True self-worth isn't built by snowplowing your child's road. It's built day by day and moment by moment on the

ABCs of *attitude*, *behavior*, and *character*. When all is said and done, those three things are what matter most in raising your son. The ABCs are what make your child kind and respectful—or not. Honest—or not. Trustworthy—or not.

It's All about Attitude

How many times can you count hearing these phrases in your house: "But I don't wanna!" and "You're not gonna make me!"

Life is all about attitude, isn't it? Do you tend to think of a glass as half empty or half full? What kids see is what they're going to adopt. Do you approach challenges with "Well, let's see how we can tackle that and overcome it," or with "Oh, no, it's just one more thing to do. I'm already overwhelmed"?

Your attitude is displayed loudly in your son's attitude, and your son's attitude is the entrance into his head and heart. Want to know what your son thinks about himself? Just listen to his mumblings sometime.

Want to know what your son thinks about himself? Just listen to his mumblings sometime.

"Man, I'm so dumb. How come I can't get it?" he might say.

That's a big clue to how your son views himself.

Attitude also comes from what happens to your son. He might have had a horrible day at school, where the guy he thought was his buddy one-upped him. Maybe what happened wasn't fair, but your child can still choose his attitude.

Attitude can speak loudly, even if your child says nothing. Nothing screams louder than the silent treatment, does it,

What This Mom Did Right

My son's a biter. When he doesn't get what he wants, he bites. My husband, my other son, and I all have had teeth marks in our arms since Sean was a baby. I tried everything I could think of to stop him from biting—even spanking. But it didn't stop. He was four and still biting. He even bit the sweet neighbor girl, who never hurt a fly!

Then I heard you talk on the radio, Dr. Leman, about how kids will seek attention, even if it's negative. That gave me an idea. The next time he bit my other son, I picked Sean up from his chair, carried him outside the door (we live in Florida and it was nice weather), placed him in the rocker in our screened-in porch, locked the outside door, and shut the door to the house. Then we calmly proceeded to have dinner, in spite of his muffled screaming and banging on the door. About 40 minutes later, when we were just clearing the dishes after having dessert, I heard a quiet tap on the door and a little voice said, "Can I come in now, Mommy?"

Sean walked in quietly. I fed him dinner (he sat by himself) and then put him to bed.

The next night his brother did something he didn't like, and Sean leaned over to bite him. But then he stopped and frowned. He looked quickly at me and pleaded, "Mommy, don't put me on the porch ever again." He ate his dinner politely and quietly.

It's been six months now, and Sean just turned five. He's never bitten any-one since that day I got the courage to put him out by himself on the porch.

Thanks, Dr. Leman! Without you I'd never have had the guts to do it.

Melanie, Florida

Mom? And especially with a woman's penchant for verbal discussion, that one can drive any mom bonkers.

A negative attitude shows itself through whining, kicking, complaining, sassing, rolling eyes, being stubborn, and insisting on things his way. It's the "me, me, me" syndrome— "everything's about me." If your son is operating this way, it has to stop. It's impacting not only him but also you and the rest of your family.

How can you nip it in the bud? It all starts with you, Mom, since you're likely the one with your son most of the time. Let's face it—even working-outside-the-home mothers are the ones running to school on their lunch hour. How many dads do you see doing that?

So when your kid cops an attitude about doing something, how do you respond?

"I said do it," you say firmly.

You get no response. Your kid might as well be deaf.

"I said do it NOW!" you say with a lot more force.

Still no action.

So what's next, Mom? Are you going to physically pick up your 80-pound son and *make* him do it? It might work with your toddler, but it won't change his attitude. His look of defiance and kicking legs will say it all.

But what if *your* attitude changes? What if you remain calm and don't nag him anymore after you ask him once? What if, instead, there is a consequence that you will put into play if he doesn't do what is expected of him?

Stay tuned for more. . . .

Acting Up

Your son's attitude has everything to do with how he behaves. How loudly is his attitude speaking?

Boys are physical, and when they get angry, they punch things, break things, slam doors, and stomp out of the room. They yell, call you names, and retreat to their messy room. Other times they narrow their eyes, cross their arms across their chest, and give you that "there's no way I'm gonna do that and you can't make me" look that makes your blood boil.

How is it that your kids can be perfect angels at Grandma's, then turn into hellions as soon as you pick them up?

Why do you think your kids act up?

The number one reason is to get your attention. They're trying to make a point through their body language. And if you don't get it, they'll ramp up the behavior just a notch.

I saw that happen the other day in the grocery store. A little boy who looked about four years old was sitting in one of those car carts, where the child can pretend like he's driving himself while Mom hurries through the store to pick up groceries. Even though the mom had made an attempt at entertainment—getting the child a fun cart—the boy wasn't placated. Every aisle they passed, he reached out for a particular item, insisting that he just had to have it. His mom said a firm no and went on.

How is it that your kids can be perfect angels at Grandma's, then turn into hellions as soon as you pick them up?

So the boy began to fuss more loudly and started to cry.

His mom ignored him and went on with her list.

He cried louder.

She ignored him.

He started to kick. His cries would stop every once in a while as he'd take a peek at her.

She ignored him.

He started thrashing.

And you know what that mom did? She raised her eyebrows and walked down the aisle to pick up something on her list . . . and away from her screaming child.

Although she was only a few feet away, it might as well have been a mile to that young boy. The screaming lessened.

When the mom lingered by the baking section, then made a move to step around the corner, the screaming stopped. The boy crawled out of the little car window and came running. "Mommy, Mommy, don't forget me!"

Ah, now there's a smart mom. I'd like to think that she's heard me speak or read one of my books.

You see, there's a purpose for every behavior. Children act a certain way only if it serves some purpose—if they get what they want. When they don't get what they want, the behavior stops. Simple enough?

> *Children act a certain way only if it serves some purpose.*

Kids are kids. You might as well accept the fact that they'll say and do the dumbest and most embarrassing things you can imagine. And they'll do them in places you wish they wouldn't, like in the middle of the grocery store. But it's the smart mom who doesn't let her kid get away with them.

Every Kid's Got Character . . . and He Might Be a Character Too

Whoever first said, "Character's not everything, it's the only thing," sure hit the nail on the head. Character is who you are when no one's looking.

Is your child kindhearted or mean-spirited? Does he help others who need help or sit back and watch them wallow? Does he give the extra quarter in his pocket to the new kid who doesn't have enough money for lunch? Is your son respectful to you, his teachers, and others in authority? Does he go out of his way to help his sister? Does he stick up for other kids on the playground?

Being a person of character doesn't mean you never do anything wrong. No human is perfect. But when a person of character does something wrong, they feel a check in their gut until they make things right. They have the courage and the integrity to go to the other person, admit what they did wrong, apologize, ask for forgiveness, and move on.

Does your son have that kind of character? Or would teachers say of him, "Oh, *that* boy. Now he's a real character. I'm sure glad I don't have him in *my* class"?

When raising your son, focus on the three things that matter most both now and in the long run: his attitude, his behavior, and his character.

Did You Know?

There's a well-hidden fact that you need to know: fighting is an act of cooperation.

Did you hear that? Fighting is an act of cooperation. After all, it takes two to battle it out. You can't exactly fight with yourself, now can you?

When your son engages you in a fight, he's doing so for a reason. He wants your attention. And if he can't get your attention in a positive way, he'll do it in a negative way.

Here's something else you need to know: when you do battle with your son, you will *never* win. You may think you do sometimes—when the kid caves in and does what you want—but underneath it all, you've lost. That's because you have a lot more to lose than your son does. Is he embarrassed if his jeans are slung so low you can see his underwear? Nope, because that's how all the guys are wearing them. (Now, you? You feel like running up from behind him and depantsing him, just so he knows how stupid he looks.) Especially since you're the one who puts up with the clucking elderly neighbor every morning who shakes her head at you for being such a rotten parent.

Let me be clear. As soon as you enter a power struggle with your son—no matter his age—you will lose.

But there's a better way—and you'll *always* win.

Do You Have Your Son's Number?

Children are creatures of habit. They like routine. They like knowing what's going to happen, when it's going to happen, and how it's going to happen. (This is particularly true of firstborns.)

Take Aaron, for example, who can't go to sleep until every stuffed animal known to humankind is lined up just so on his bed. It's a 45-minute routine.

> *There's a better way—and you'll always win.*

Or Alvin, who keeps his school schedule by his bed so he can look at it every morning and know exactly what he's doing for the day.

Then there's Corey, who knows that his family has spaghetti every Wednesday night, and he counts on it.

When your son tries out a behavior, he thinks, *Let's see if this works.*

Then, *Hey, it does work! Mom came running! Cool! Hmm, let's see if it works again . . .*

Hey, it worked. I got her attention. This is fun.

And that particular behavior becomes a part of your child's experience because it accomplished its *purposive behavior*—it got your attention, Mom.

But what if that behavior is something you want to change?

It's simple. You choose to no longer walk into your son's trap. When his behavior no longer works, he'll stop doing it!

Now, will this happen instantly? No, it will take follow-through and consistency on your part. You can't back down or you'll lose your edge, and you'll have to start all over again. So make it easier on yourself. Stick to your guns and *don't back down.* The more entrenched this behavior is in your child, the longer it will take to change it, but if you don't waffle, you'll be surprised at how you capture his attention.

> *When his behavior no longer works, he'll stop doing it!*

How does it work?

It All Starts with a Reality Check

I love goldfish as pets. If you don't feed them, they die. (Okay, no fish were actually harmed in this example. I'm not really telling you to buy a fish and let it die.) Nothing like a little visible reminder to make a child be responsible.

"But, Dr. Leman, that's *horrible!*" you say. "It'll damage my son's psyche to see his pet fish floating dead in the fish tank!"

Oh really? Then it'll be an even better reminder to your son to feed and care for the next pet he has. It's called *responsibility.* If a child can't handle a little responsibility like feeding a pinch of food a day to a goldfish, how do you think he's going to handle keeping track of his homework? Or arriving on time to his first job? Or anything else in life that takes responsibility?

If your son doesn't do something he should, he suffers the consequence of that action. And if he acts in a way that he shouldn't, he bears the consequence for that too. After all, isn't that the way real life works? Cushioning your child from the consequences of his actions isn't reality; it's creating for him a Disneyland experience that's pure fantasy.

The fact that actions have consequences is a valuable, basic lesson that children must learn through observation and experience.

Let's say your 10-year-old son begs and begs to stay up late. (To him, that means 10:30 p.m.) Instead of giving him the lecture about how tired he'll be the next day if he does so, let him stay up one night to see what it feels like.

But when he's dragging the next morning, don't cut him any slack. Insist that he follow the same routine he always does during the day and that he keeps going until bedtime. No naps allowed. Bet it'll be a long time before your son begs to stay up late again. Even better, you didn't have to deliver a lecture or say a word, did you? (Other than "Okay" in response to his plea to stay up late.)

Your home needs to be a place where your son can fail—and learn from that failure.

Look what a smart mom you are.

Too many times moms feel empathetic and try to rescue their offspring from trouble. But if you do that, you don't do your son the favor of learning from his mistakes. That means he'll be likely to do the same thing again. After all, when you rescue him and continue to rescue him, that's all part of the game of getting your attention.

Your home needs to be a place where your son can fail—and learn from that failure—not a place where he's continually rescued from his own dumb moves. So let your son experience a little reality. It isn't your job to get your kid off the hook for the dumb things he does. In fact, your job is to keep your son *on* the hook so he learns what it's like to struggle on it and figure a way to get himself off it. Your son's smart. Once he's floundered on that hook for a while, it's not as likely he'll let himself get caught by it again.

Don't Let Your Emotions Get the Better of You

I know what you feel like, because I've been there too. Sometimes you just want to wring your kid's neck, and you speak or act without thinking first.

When Tricia got a call from her son's private-school office that her son had been caught smoking behind the junior high gym, she was stunned. Her jaw dropped further when she found out he was the one who had illegally purchased the cigarettes for all his buddies to try. The first thought that sprang to her mind was, *What are you, an IDIOT?*

But thankfully, she just said to the school secretary, "Thanks for letting me know. I'll be right there," and made her way to school. Even better, it was a 20-minute drive, so she had time to cool down and think through her options.

The mom who walked into the principal's office wasn't the mom Cole expected. This mom was calm and confident and agreed with everything the principal said. Cole was put on probation and given a job: for two weeks, he had to stay after school and clean every classroom's blackboard.

Sometimes you just want to wring your kid's neck.

When they drove home, Tricia waited for Cole to say something. He scrooched uncomfortably for about 10 minutes, then blurted out, "Aren't you going to yell at me or something?" He couldn't handle her calm and quietness.

115

She was quiet a few more minutes, then said, "I'd like to talk with you about it after dinner."

That boy had three more hours to be miserable and think about his actions before he and his mom talked in the den.

"Son," she began, "I was disappointed to hear not only that you chose to smoke but that you bought cigarettes illegally. Worse, you passed them out to the other guys and got them in trouble too."

She went on to tell him she'd decided that before he was allowed to get together with any friends or play any games on the computer, he would write a 10-page research paper for her on the harms of smoking. It would include a bibliography and quotes from a minimum of 10 internet sources.

Cole looked at her in shock, as if in disbelief that his mom was so rational. And she wasn't yelling.

It took Cole, who struggled with writing papers, three weeks to complete that assignment. In the meantime, he was embarrassed to explain to his buddies why he couldn't go to the movie they'd planned on Friday night or out for pizza the next week.

Ten years have passed since that day. Today Cole is 23, but he vividly remembers that paper. "I was never tempted to smoke again," he says and grins. "After that, I knew Mom meant business. Even though Dad was no longer around, I sure didn't run Mom around the block anymore."

After Cole got over the immediate shock, he admired his mom's gutsiness—even if it did take him until after college to admit it to her.

The smart mom will learn how to respond rather than react. *Responding* means you take all the information in, think about it awhile, then decide how you're going to act for the child's best interest. *Reacting* means you jump to do and say the first thing that comes to mind. You act without thinking through all the consequences first. That's why you hear moms saying, "You'll *never* get to do that again!" but then a week (or a day or an hour) later, they relent and let their child do that same thing.

Don't fall into the guilt trap of thinking you're being too hard on the poor boy. He'll live, and he'll be better off for you not backing down. When Cole's mom said she was disappointed in what had happened, that raked coals over her kid's head. As the old adage says, "Nobody's happy when mama ain't happy."

Sometimes kids need to get in touch with their feelings—they need to experience some good, healthy guilt for what they've done wrong, and they need to feel uncomfortable. It's all a part of growth.

When you *respond*, you stay in the driver's seat and stay focused on the direction you're heading. When you *react*, you let your child get into the driver's seat and drive to wherever he wants to go.

That puts things bluntly in perspective, doesn't it?

B Doesn't Happen Until A Is Completed

Sometimes your son will just be grumpy and angry. He'll be set to do battle with someone. And he'll have his eye on you as the prime target.

But you don't have to fall for it. Disengage yourself from the battle. Remember we talked about how it takes two to fight? Your son is 11 years old, so he has an excuse. He's just learning the ropes of life and relationships. You're the adult here. You're 33, so you don't have an excuse. Act like an adult and take charge.

If your son wants to be grumpy and angry, let him be grumpy and angry. In fact, let him be miserable if he wants. It's not your job to make your child happy. As I've said before, "An unhappy child is a healthy child." Why's that? Because an unhappy child isn't getting his way all the time; he's learning that sometimes life isn't all about him. And that will lead him to be a healthier adult.

But here's the kicker. Just because your son is acting the way he is doesn't mean that he gets off not doing what he's supposed to. If he's unhappy, he can be unhappy as he cleans his room, rakes leaves, or mows the lawn. Whatever he's supposed to be doing at that time, he still needs to do.

Just because your son is acting the way he is doesn't mean that he gets off not doing what he's supposed to.

And if he chooses not to? Then "B doesn't happen until A is completed." That means when your son shows up later for you to take him to baseball, and his room still isn't clean or the leaves aren't raked or the lawn isn't mowed, you don't take him. He can complain or yell all he wants, but the car simply doesn't travel that direction, no matter how much he begs or bats those baby blues at you. End of story.

Do you think next time your son will adjust his attitude? Especially when he has to take grief from the coach and his fellow players for not showing up? (By the way, you don't snowplow his road by calling the coach to explain what happened. You let him take care of that himself. He's the one who put himself on the hot seat, so he might as well enjoy every aspect of it.)

And you? You didn't even break a sweat arguing. You just stuck to the principle of "B doesn't happen until A is completed," and now your son knows you mean business.

Will your son test you again? Sure. That's only human nature. In fact, he might ramp it up next time to see if you really do mean business. (This is especially true if you've backed down a lot before.) But if you consistently follow that principle, you'll find that your son will test you less and less because now *he's* got something to lose. And he sure doesn't want to explain that to his buddies.

Blabbermouths Anonymous

Children can be notoriously "mommy deaf." After you've spewed so many words their direction, they've learned to tune you out. They figure that when you raise your voice to a certain notch (after about the third request you've made of them), then you really mean business and they better pay attention. But they're trained not to respond until after you reach that certain decibel, just a few levels below a screech, and then they hop to it.

What if, instead, you presented your request just once?

"I have a project I have to get done before tomorrow, so I'd like you to make dinner tonight," you say to your son. "I put everything to make spaghetti on the counter. The rest is up to you."

Then you turn your back and walk away, back to the project you have to finish.

An hour later, you note that it's 6:00, and you still don't smell dinner cooking.

An hour passes. Still no spaghetti.

It's 7:20. Still no spaghetti.

At 7:30 you microwave yourself a meal, take it into your office, shut the door, and go back to work.

At 7:35, your son pokes his nose into your office. "Uh, Mom? Aren't we having dinner? I'm getting hungry."

Don't Let Your Son Push Your Buttons

- Say it once.
- Turn your back.
- Walk away.

It works every time.

You calmly reply, "I'm having dinner right now. Your dinner is on the counter."

"But, Mom, I'm really hungry. Can't you—"

You get up, shut the door, and go back to work.

It's about 8:15 when you finally smell spaghetti in the kitchen and hear the annoyed voices of your son's siblings. You smile to yourself. Spaghetti sure would have tasted better than your Lean Cuisine frozen dinner, but you made your point. Your child still had to make dinner for himself and his siblings, just like you asked. Even if it took a few extra hours.

It's amazing what can happen when your kids learn that you will only say things once.

Follow Through on Your Word

If you say that something is going to happen, make it happen. No wishy-washiness. No "I'm too tired to follow through." Your son's got your number, and if you don't follow through on what you said you'd do, he'll test you to see how far he can push you.

If you say, "You have to finish your science project for the fair before you can play Xbox," don't back down. The science project gets done first. If your son sneaks behind your back and plays Xbox anyway, he loses his Xbox privileges for that night and the next week.

Mom, don't back down. When you say something is going to happen, it has to happen. God didn't put you on this earth to be run over by your kid.

Love and discipline—you can't have one without the other.

Love and discipline—you can't have one without the other.

Expect the Best

"We're going to the mall, Jarod, and when we do, I want you to be good," you admonish as you're tucking your three-year-old into his car seat.

What have you just told your child? "Jarod, when we get to the store, I'm expecting you to act up. So I'm just warning you now you better not."

What you expect is most often what you get. No wonder so many kids are throwing tantrums in public. Their moms expect it of them!

When you expect the best out of your son, you're more likely to get it. When your child behaves wonderfully, tell him, "Jarod, I love it when we can do things together, just you and Mommy. It was fun to go to the mall together today, wasn't it? Maybe we can do that some other time. You were so patient about waiting to ride on the cars so I could do a little shopping. I appreciate that. Do you want your favorite—a cheese and jelly sandwich—for a snack now?" What are you doing? You're reinforcing your son's good behavior by telling him how much you appreciated his actions at the mall, and you're treating him to his favorite snack as a result. Do you think that child is going to be well-behaved again at the mall, remembering the results? You bet! In addition, you're enhancing the closeness of your relationship.

What You Can Do

- Focus on your child's attitude, behavior, and character.
- Expect the best, and you're more likely to get it.
- Remember that without discipline, there is no love.

So say no to daily battles with your son. You're smarter than that.

A ll of you reading this book are at a different place in the journey.

Some of you are pregnant, expecting your first child. Some are wading through adoption papers. Others of you are already holding that infant or toddler in your arms.

Still others are going through that traumatic transition to preschool or kindergarten.

Some of you are discovering what homework in fourth grade is like.

Others have just begun that eye-opening phase called adolescence.

Some of you are holding on with your fingernails as your child learns how to drive.

Others of you are brushing back tears, as your son will soon graduate from high school.

Some of you have come a long way; others still have a long way to go.

The next two chapters address various ages and stages of life with your child, so read the ones that apply to you. (It's okay if you take a peek at the other ones too!)

6

Ages and Stages #1

From Infant and Toddler to Early School Age

Each step in the journey of growing up has its joys . . . and its challenges. Here's how you can get off to a great start and make the best of this time of transition.

There's nothing like getting plunged into parenting, is there?

If you birthed your son, you went to Lamaze class, watched your stomach swell to incredible proportions, and suffered through backaches, but they were nothing like the pangs of childbirth, where you gripped your doctor's arm like it was a lifeline and yelled, "I need drugs!"

If you adopted your son, you went through months or years of paperwork and endured fingerprinting like you were some

criminal, numerous blood tests, and several adoption con-
sultants scrutinizing you to see if you would be a good mom.
You thought the worst was over, didn't you?

Then you arrive home, 36 hours after the blessed event,
all starry-eyed over your new son. You've left the "experts"
at the hospital behind, and now all you have is a diaper
bag of tools you're not quite sure how to use. Then your
beloved son starts crying, and you can't get him to stop.
What's wrong? you wonder. *Why can't
I fix it? Am I a terrible mother?*

You thought the worst was over, didn't you?

Take it from a grizzled veteran of five
kids, you'll make mistakes. You'll often
wonder about your parenting skills. But
you'll also discover things such as dirt
doesn't kill, a child who misses a meal will not die, and everybody gets diarrhea.

Here's what you have to understand. This little 19.5-incher
you're holding in your arms will rather quickly develop into
a real, full-functioning, little person. One of the few things
you can get psychiatrists, psychologists, and counselors to
agree on is that your child's personality forms in his first
several years of life. That doesn't mean your child doesn't
come with an inherent temperament. Some kids are feisty
from the get-go, and others are as docile as a stuffed animal.
But how you interact with that child is going to make a huge
difference in how he views life both now and in the future.

Anne Ortlund once said, "Children are wet cement." I've
always liked that word picture because if you've ever watched
anyone pour cement, you know that it's very malleable. It
flows easily. Any kid I know is intensely tempted to carve
their initials on it. And like cement, your son's personality
starts to harden up and form.

Memo to Moms

All babies cry. That's what babies do. In fact, they need to cry. It strengthens their lungs, and it's a part of human experience. The smart mom won't panic. She'll learn to discern her baby's cries:

"I'm in pain!"
"I want some attention—*now!*"
"I'm hungry."
"I'm wet."

Then she'll know how to respond appropriately.

Get Ready, Get Set, Go!

Your game plan for the first ten days with your child? It's simple. Survival! New babies don't sleep on a schedule. You can try, but you won't establish one right away. Instead, your nights will become days and your days nights, until your son adjusts to living outside of your womb. So do yourself a favor. Nap when your child naps, even if it's 10 minutes at a time. Don't worry about dust bunnies in your corner or your mother-in-law coming over and seeing your bad housekeeping. Your priority is to take care of yourself and your son.

Life at this stage is pretty simple. When your son is wet or poopy, change him. When he's hungry, feed him. Believe me, you won't have to wonder when these things happen. You'll smell him or hear him, or he'll announce them loudly and clearly. Your baby will sleep a lot, and he needs to sleep a lot.

During this stage, it's crucial that you bond with your baby skin to skin. Whether you're breast-feeding or not, place your baby right against your skin, by your breasts. There's no warmer, safer, or more comfortable place in the world for a baby than to be tucked closely in that spot.

Make wake-up times and go-to-sleep-at-night times special bonding moments. If you were a baby, what would you want to see most when you wake up or when you're going to sleep? Mommy's smiling face makes for a good start to the day and sweet dreams for the night.

Realize Not Everyone Sees Your Son as a Good Thing

If your son is your secondborn, realize that not everyone will see bringing this baby home as a good thing. Your firstborn, in fact, may see him as a little intruder—especially if the two children are close in age. All of a sudden the firstborn's privileged status as the only child in the family who got all the attention from you has disappeared, and this *thing* is the reason why. No wonder you often hear stories about older siblings biting the baby or hitting him on the head with a shoe. That's exactly how they feel.

So as you bond with your baby, take some time out with your firstborn. Tell him how special he is to you and that as the "big boy," he has special privileges. Your firstborn needs to be assured that even with the arrival of this new little one, his place in the family is secure.

The First Year

For most moms, the first year is a year of ups and downs, a year of exhaustion and emotional and hormonal changes. You might even get the baby blues—emotional mood swings that make your husband enemy number one—and find it difficult to muster up energy to take care of your baby. Realize that these swings are normal, and this too will pass. During these times, make sure you have a support network. Take a walk.

Go to the grocery store by yourself. Take a long shower. Talk to your doctor about what you're experiencing, and see if he or she can help in any way.

Take it easy, Mom. Use this first year to bond with your baby. Read to him, nestle him against your breasts and in your lap. Say no to outside activities as much as possible. There will never be another year like this one.

During this year, your child will fall more naturally into a schedule of eating and sleeping.

A Smart Step

The discipline that you start out with on day one becomes a part of your child's life. The smartest thing any couple can do upon that little 19.5-incher's arrival is to go out for an evening by themselves.

"What?" you're saying. "Are you kidding? You think I'm going to leave this little baby all by himself and go out? Are you crazy?"

No, I'm a psychologist. And I'm right. You and your husband need to go out and leave your child with a qualified babysitter. Grandma will do, and then some.

Going out sets the tone for your relationship both now and in the future. Your son needs to learn that Mom and Dad won't always be here and that you need mini-vacations from him—even if that mini-vacation is only two and a half hours long. You're also saying, "I love you, but I also love your daddy, and it's important for me to spend time with him." It builds healthy boundaries that will help your entire family. Any daddy who has his needs fulfilled will be much happier and willing to help with anything that needs to be done at home.

Talking, Walking, and Potty Training

Every child talks and walks on a different schedule, so don't compare your son with anyone else. He is who he is, and unless there's a physical problem, he will walk and talk in his own time. Those are natural functions, just like sleeping, eating, and going potty.

I need to ask you something. Chances are good that you've gone potty today, but does someone give you an M&M every time you go potty? No? Then why should you do that with your son? Parents are great at fabricating schemes to get their kids to do what comes naturally.

When you say, "Oh, Frank! Mikey has just gone poopy. Oh, come and look. Isn't that great?" what's your son thinking? *Boy, that wasn't so hard. One grunt and a four-and-a-half-incher plopped out. These people will do anything for entertainment. Let's see now, if next time . . .*

If you make a big deal about potty training, it will become a big deal. Treat it as just a natural thing that you do and it takes all the challenge out of it. Instead of pushing potty training, look for signs of readiness: interest in a big potty, dislike of wet or poopy diapers and the way they feel, etc. The time to strike is when a child's interested. Then be calm about it.

Uh-Oh, He's a Toddler

Now's the time to ask yourself, *What do I want my son to be like when he grows up?* Because it all starts right here, Mom. If you want your child to be responsible, to care about others, and to share your moral and spiritual values, the training begins in these years.

Why does your child behave a certain way? Because it serves a purpose in his life. He gets something from it. Your son will "try on" behaviors to see what works—and he'll continue those that work.

Take these common statements your son might make at bedtime, after you've tucked him into bed and started to walk out of his room:

"Mommy, I want a snack. I'm hungry."

"Water, water, I want water."

"There's a monster in my closet, and he's got green eyes and fire coming out of his mouth! He's going to get me!"

What is your son doing? Back to the purposive behavior. What does your child want? He wants to delay his bedtime. He wants your presence just a little bit longer. He already had a snack, so he's workin' ya. If you heed those requests, he'll ask you night after night after night, and the requests and time involved will only ramp up.

But what about his fear of monsters? Yes, it's his imagination, but it can also be very real to your son. So get creative. Think of a solution. One of my favorites is putting a squirt bottle (empty, of course) by the child's bed and saying, "Well, if that monster peeks out his head, you can just squirt this magic bottle, and he'll go away! So you have nothing to worry about."

What about the kid who pops out of bed like a toaster pastry time after time when you've already tucked him in?

It's All in the Perspective

Jill Savage, head of Hearts at Home, told me a wonderful story. As a mom, she was exhausted. She never seemed to have time to herself. One morning she got up early, when everyone else was still asleep, and said to herself, *I'm going to go downstairs and just enjoy some quiet time by myself.*

But as soon as she was settled in her chair, she was acutely aware of little footsteps coming toward her. Her son, who was two or three at the time, looked up at her.

"Mommy," he said, "have you been waiting for me?"

The old adage is true: how you handle life's little interruptions has everything to do with your perspective.

Don't fall for that one, Mom! When your son goes to bed, you need time to yourself. So pick him up without saying a word, put him back in bed, and close the door. When you do, he'll likely scream like a stuck pig. He'll run to the door and try to open it. But you're holding on to the other side. (For those of you saying, "Dr. Leman, how could you? That's cruel! Not going to your child when he needs you?" and wanting to tear up this book right now, just give me a minute before you pass judgment.) He'll rattle the door, kick it, and have a regular hissy fit. But you don't say a single word. Everything in you wants to say, "Knock it off! And get in bed!" As soon as you do that, though, you've given your son what he was after. You've given a reaction. He's involved you in his behavior, which means he's won.

So even though you're tired and frustrated, you continue to hold the door shut. When he's quiet (usually a first attempt will be a little less than 10 minutes), open the door gently. He might break your heart because he's curled up behind the door with his blankie under his arm. If he's strong willed, he might give the protest one more shot as soon as he sees you. But this time, don't close the door. Just say quietly, "Honey,

I'll leave the door open, but you need to stay in bed. If you don't stay in bed, I'll close the door."

"Mommy," he'll plead, "leave the light on."

"I won't leave the light on, but the night-light is plugged in. You have to stay in bed."

For those of you who think I'm cruel, consider this: do you want to win the battle with your son right there, or do you want to fight the same battle over and over again *for years*? That is up to you by the way you handle this situation.

Sharing

Your son won't naturally share. After all, all children start out with the perspective of "me, me, me, and only me." He needs to be taught to share by you demonstrating. Before he's three, make sure that even if your child is an only child, you share things with him, and then ask him to share things with you. "See, Nathan, Mommy shares with you. Grandma shares with you. Sometimes you need to share with [whomever he's with]." By the time your child hits age three, he should be taught how to share, take turns, compete (nicely), and work with others. If your son turns three and four and still doesn't understand sharing, get more aggressive about it. If he can't share a toy, then remove the toy so he can't play with it either. If he doesn't understand waiting his turn in line, explain, "Honey, we need to wait. See the other people in line in front of us? That little girl and her mommy will get her popcorn, then the man will get his, and then it's our turn." If your child doesn't have siblings, preschool can be a good place to learn those lessons. If your son doesn't go to preschool, scheduling playtimes with a number of children will help to ease this process.

How to Make a Monster

If you overreact to things that happen, you'll turn them into power struggles. Parents with PhDs make fools of themselves with a child's spoon, trying to trick that child into eating: "Here's the plane, honey; open up wide for the plane!"

As soon as the plane enters the airspace directly in front of the kid's mouth, his lips clench shut. The hangar is closed! Do you think that child has your number? Your son has to eat sometime. If you don't try to make him eat, he will eat when he gets hungry. So don't cajole. Simply remove the food. If your child asks for food 10 minutes later, wait awhile before you serve it again. If the child is older, wait until the next meal and tell him the kitchen is closed until then.

The same goes for the time your son pulls a temper tantrum in Walgreens when you won't give him the Tootsie Pop he's asked for, and he literally throws himself on the floor and goes at it. Worse, four adults are standing there in the aisle, staring wide-eyed at you and your child. What should you do? Step over your son. (Yes, you'll be tempted to step *on* him, but don't do it. You're more mature than that.) Then look the other adults straight in the eye and say, "Well! Some people's children!" As you move away and start to turn the corner, guess who will stop the tantrum and come running? That's because his behavior didn't work and he doesn't want to be separated from you.

A note to those of you who have allowed this behavior to go on for two, three, or four years. The longer your child has been playing this game, the tougher it will be to stop it. But with all due respect, now's the time to make a change. Do you want to battle your son until he graduates from college? Or do you want a respectful, thoughtful, non-self-centered son?

A Lot of Mommy

In these early years, your son needs a lot of Mommy. That's why it's critical that you think carefully through what activities you can do and can't do outside the home. At first, your son won't be able to do anything by himself. He can't change his diaper or feed himself. As he grows, he'll start saying things like, "By self."

Take your clue from your son's words. He wants to do as many things as possible by himself now. He's changing, growing, maturing. So be a good observer of your son.

Boys usually mature later than girls. (Just take a look at fifth graders if you don't believe me. Many of the girls will be developed to look like young women, but boys will still look like little boys.) If your son is physically small or he's a late-birthday-in-the-year baby, it's not a bad idea to start him a year later in kindergarten. That will give him more of a competitive edge in the tough world of boys, where physical size and strength is an important thing. (No boy wants to be the wimp who gets creamed.) It will also give him another year at home to hone his social skills, since boys are often more socially and emotionally immature than girls.

I've spent a lot of this chapter on the years of infancy through age five or six, because these years, before a child goes to kindergarten, are critically important. During these foundational years, when you are a huge influence in your child's life (and oftentimes the only regular influence in his day, at least until he goes to preschool), strive for consistent action. If you say something is going to happen, make it happen. Don't coax or remind. Let your child discover, even as a toddler, that if he doesn't do what you ask him to do, there are consequences. And above all, don't do things for your son that he can do for himself. Allow him to learn to respect himself, whether he can do many things or just a few.

Kindergarten Woes

It's been well recorded by both my mother and older sister, Sally, that I cried for the first two weeks of kindergarten. (In those days, there wasn't any preschool, so kindergarten was really the first time I was away from my mother.) In fact, I cried so much in the afternoon class that I had to be moved to the morning class so my big sister could take me to school. I remember her putting me on her big bike—I couldn't reach the pedals—as she and her girlfriend escorted me to school in the morning. Such treatment dried up my tears enough to finally make the transition.

Many children are excited about getting to kindergarten, where they can play with other kids (they haven't yet figured out that there will be some work there too). Others are clingy and fearful about leaving you. Either way, kindergarten is a huge change in the life of both mom and child. It's your son's first time to be "on his own." The best thing you can do to help the transition is to take your son with you to what I call the "warm-up day," where you can visit the school and the classroom and meet the teacher. If your son is going to ride on the bus, the school often even has the parent and child ride it together to get used to the route and know how to get to the classroom from the bus.

On the first day of school, just about every child will suffer a little separation anxiety. The cleaner the break, Mom, the better. Don't linger to mop up any tears from your child. Just kiss and hug him good-bye, then walk out of the classroom.

A good kindergarten teacher will take his hand and help him get involved in an activity.

Most likely some of you will go around the corner and burst into tears yourself. After all, your baby is growing up, and you might not be ready for it. But others of you might be sighing in relief and going out for coffee in celebration. Life goes on.

Some kindergartens are a half day; others are a full day. Realize that your son is going to be very tired when he comes home from school. All that social interaction with new kids will wipe him out. He may be grumpy and just need some playtime. Cut him some slack. Imagine what it would feel like if you had a new job and were getting to know everybody. You'd be tired too.

Also, when your son starts school, he'll realize something: he's not the center of the universe. There are a lot of other kids there too, and some of them are bigger! He'll meet children from different neighborhoods, income classes, and ethnic groups. The world suddenly becomes much bigger and wider.

The Early School Years (First through Third Grade)

First grade is a big transition too. Many children are going from half a day to a full day at school. And some schools start homework early. In first grade he'll already have a little homework. It's important to decide on and establish good work habits. Don't snowplow your son's road. Make *him* responsible for his homework. I've seen too many projects at science fairs that aren't the child's work but the parent's work, so don't fall for that. You've already been through school; now it's your son's chance.

An important note about homework: no child can go through an entire school day and then tackle homework immediately upon reaching home (unless they're driven and wired that way). Everybody needs a break. You do and your son does. So give your son a snack and allow him to take a break, but set a time when the homework needs to start. Get into a regular routine, and it won't become a battle later.

During these early school years, emphasize reading, even if your son doesn't like it at first. If your son develops good reading habits, he'll bloom at school. Reading (both in school and outside of school) needs to be high on your priority list, even for active boys who would do anything to get out of it. So find books that your son will like and make them easily accessible.

Realize that your child's social life has changed as well. He used to play all day. Now he can only play part of the day. And his friends might have changed drastically too. Go out of your way to arrange playtimes—short ones if they're during the school week—with like-minded little boys your son enjoys.

The Homework-Intensified Years
(Fourth through Fifth Grade)

During these years, school becomes more important as homework and responsibility ramp up. Many students also start music lessons at school.

During these years, attitude, behavior, and character are most important. How your son treats others says a lot about his attitude and how you're doing raising him. What does he act like when another kid is picked on? Does he join in with the bullying or defend the child being hurt? His response says a lot about his character.

In these years, children start to form cliques—groups of like-minded and like-acting children. These cliques can be very painful for those children who aren't included. Teach your son that being a member of a group can be a good thing, but it's not if it excludes and demeans other children. Encourage him to enjoy his friends but to keep his friendships wide and to always be kind to other people.

If your child is a little "different" from the other children, he'll experience what it's like to be the odd man out and how mean a peer group can be. If this is happening to your son at school, go out of your way to have other boys over (one at a time) to play and get to know your son. Also, widen his horizons so that he's not playing just with other children from school.

Keeping Grades in Perspective

Every mom wants her child to do well. Does that mean your son should always get As in everything? Every child has different gifts and abilities, different strengths and weaknesses. Don't expect As out of your C+ son. But do expect his best—that he studies hard for tests, that he pays attention in the classroom, that he asks for help when he doesn't understand something. Encourage your child with statements like, "Honey, it's good to see that you enjoy learning. And it looks like all that extra work you did on your science project really paid off. I bet that grade makes you feel good inside." Notice in this statement that you're not praising the child: "Oh, you're such a good boy. You got an A!" Instead, your statement reflects the fact that the child has worked hard and

---

What This Mom Did Right

My mom was a tough old bird. I came into her life when she was 42 (one of those late-in-life surprise babies), my brother was 13, and my sister was 15. I'll never forget the day I tried to talk my sister, Vanessa, into doing my chores. I was 8, and I thought I was doing a good job of it until Mom whipped around the corner. "Franklin!" she said, frowning (I can still hear the tone in her voice to this day). "It's your job. *You* do it."

My mom was like that. I tried to wiggle out of things, but she held me accountable. When I decided I hated reading, she took me to the library the next day, made me check out a book, and said I had the weekend to read it. I groaned, but I did it. I knew my mama. She always got her way and she never backed down, but she was never mean, just firm. I knew my mom loved me.

Five years later, my mom died of a rare blood disease that we didn't even know she had. I'd give anything now to hear her whip around the corner today and say, "Franklin!" with that same tone she once used to set me straight. And it worked. I'm a different man today than I would have been if I hadn't had my mom's influence early on in my life.

Franklin, Oregon

---

his effort has paid off. Your child will thrive and excel on that kind of encouragement.

Remember that grades reflect only *one* type of learning. Your son may be good at memorizing lists or terrible at it. He may get an A in science lab but flunk the written tests. We all learn differently. Help your child find and hone the natural ways he learns.

Hold Your Child Accountable

When you forget to put gas in your car, whose fault is it? And when you forget to pay a bill and you're charged a late fee on the next bill, whose fault is it?

Keep the ball of consequences on your son's side of the tennis court. If he is taking clarinet lessons in fourth grade but forgets his clarinet and heads off to school with his buddies, don't rescue him. Let him be the one to explain to the band instructor why he doesn't have it. I guarantee that he'll have it the next class. If your child insists he wants to play the trumpet but three weeks into it decides he wants to quit, say no. If a child commits to something himself, he should stick with it for at least a semester. Then, if he still doesn't like it after that semester, he can try something else. But allowing your son to start and stop things willy-nilly isn't teaching him anything.

I tried to learn how to play the trumpet in fourth grade and only got as far as "Rock of Ages" before both my mom and I decided that enough was enough. Music was not my thing. How very well I remember being in the church choir. The director, who had a PhD in music, said, "Kevin, do you realize you're singing two octaves too low?"

And I said, "What's an octave?"

I have five children, and in all their growing-up years, I never once asked any of them, "Do you have any homework tonight?" Why should you ask? It's your son's homework, not yours. So hold him accountable to do his homework. And if he doesn't, let his teacher be the one to set him straight. Does that mean you shouldn't be involved if your child asks for help? No. If your child truly needs help, find an older child who can tutor him on a hard subject after school, or a teacher who is willing to give some extra help during lunch hour. But don't ever do your son's homework for him.

> *It's your son's homework, not yours.*

The Activity Trap

With more homework during these years, you need to be especially careful about how many activities you allow your

The Leman Family Rule

One activity per kid per semester.
No exceptions.

child to be involved in. In the Leman household, our rule was one activity per child per semester. That means if your child is in orchestra, he's not in soccer. If he's in Boy Scouts, he's not in baseball. One thing at a time. Keep the focus during the school year on his primary responsibility—school.

Pursuing constant after-school and weekend activities won't give your son the time he needs to just be a kid or to relax. And it makes you the family taxicab driver (in the yellow minivan), shuttling your son from door to door all in the name of what's good for Fletcher.

But it's not good for Fletcher. Some activity is good, but if there is too much of it, it takes its toll on you—your career, your marriage, your home, your sex life—and your son. Just because your son wants to do basketball, soccer, football, and karate doesn't mean he should. No one member of the family is more important than any other member of the family, or the family as a whole. Too much activity will cut down on your family time, which is what will matter in the long run. Letting your child do everything he wants is a recipe for disaster. The smart mom will discern the difference between what her son needs and what he wants.

Too often parents tend to project their unfulfilled dreams and wishes onto their children. Too many sons are playing baseball just because Daddy did or taking piano lessons just because Mom is determined they'll have some musical ability. And they hate it. Make sure the activities your child is doing are ones that *he* is interested in, and he'll be

---

What You Can Do

- Take clues from your child about what he needs from you.
- Teach him to be responsible and hold him accountable.
- Stay away from the activity trap.
- Enjoy your son! There are no years like these, where you figure so prominently in your son's life.

---

more likely to follow through on practicing without you nagging him.

Just remember—you're not training a rat that has to run down the T-maze perfectly in order to get his reward at the end. You're raising a child who needs to have the freedom at this young age to explore his likes and dislikes.

Train Up a . . . Puppy?

Some puppies are easier to train than others. Some get things right away. The others take awhile to figure out that it is to everybody's benefit to do their doodies on the grass in the backyard, not on the Berber carpet.

The same is true of children. Some sons are easy to train and raise; others will give you a run for your money.

There's a wonderful proverb that perfectly fits the ages and stages of children from infancy through grade five: "Train a child in the way he should go, and when he is old he will not turn from it."[1] These are the years, Mom, where you focus on the basics. You teach your son responsibility and accountability through consequences for his actions, rather than over-mothering him and trying to cushion him from the real world. You keep an eye on his attitude, behavior, and character. (After all, if those are shaping up nicely, you have nothing to worry about in the long run, even if you do have

143

a few surprises along the way.) And most of all, you limit activities so you can spend time with your son.

You've done a lot of work already in raising this son from his early years to where he is now. Why not take a little joy in watching the process along the way? This is a rich time of change and exploration. I guarantee someday you'll have some anecdotes about your son to share around the family dinner table that will make him laugh . . . and remember with fondness his growing-up years.

7

Ages and Stages #2

From Middle School to High School

*Each step in the journey of growing up has its
joys . . . and its challenges. Here's how you can
make the best of both and help your child step
up to the plate on his own.*

Luke was one of those kids who kept teachers guessing.
He was always up to something, and his classmates came
to expect it. One winter day just after lunch, he sneaked out
of his seventh-grade class and into the nearby bathroom to
lock all the stalls from the inside. Then he proceeded to do the
same thing not only in the boys' bathroom but in every other
bathroom on that floor, including the one the teachers used.

An hour later the janitor figured something was up when
there were long lines at every bathroom and a lot of girls

were doing the potty dance. Somebody ratted on Luke, so he was called into the principal's office. His punishment? Staying after school for two hours and having to crawl under each bathroom stall and unlock it. If he finished, he was supposed to keep locking and unlocking stalls—"to get it out of your system," the principal said.

Adolescent boys will do really dumb things. That's a given.

Five thirty came and went. The principal went home for dinner and totally forgot about Luke being in the bathrooms, locking and unlocking stalls. When Luke's mom finally went to school at 7:30, the janitor went on a search for Luke . . . and found him still locking and unlocking the stalls! (I kind of like the kid; he reminds me of myself.)

Adolescent boys will do really dumb things. That's a given. When I was a sophomore in high school and I was at a party, somebody egged another guy on to smash me in the mouth—for no reason. The guy did, and he knocked me straight out.

A Rapidly Changing World

If you're the parent of an adolescent, you don't need me to tell you that it's a tough world out there. You pray every day that your son won't get into too much trouble, or start drinking, or get into drugs, or get killed in a car accident, or . . . The litany goes on. But the more you understand about the time I call the "critical years"—where any one decision your son makes can change the rest of his life—the better you'll be able to help your son get through them and to the other side as a healthy, well-adjusted adult.

Ah, Adolescence (the Middle School Years of Sixth through Eighth Grade)

All of a sudden the boy who's a joy to be around changes before your very eyes. He gets moody and irritable. When you're driving him to school, he says, "Hey, Mom, drop me off here."

"But, honey, we're four blocks from school!" you say.

"I want to walk the rest of the way," he says quickly.

What is he really trying to tell you? *Right now I don't want to even acknowledge that I've got a mom. It's just a little embarrassing.*

Should you be offended? No, your boy is simply ready to spread his wings. He's doing what's natural—starting to break away from you.

He's also starting to evaluate what life is all about. *Mom's taught me to believe this*, he thinks, *but is it really true?*

It's usually during this time that your son may no longer want to hug you. *Especially* around his buddies. So take the clue from your son. If you really have to hug him, do so in private.

You may have laid the foundation well for your son in his earlier years, but every adolescent gets just a little weird. If you expect it, it won't take you by surprise.

Changeability is part and parcel of growing up. If you tried to put adolescence on a graph to pictorially demonstrate what it's like, it would be a squiggly line all over the place.

That's why one minute your son may yell, "Whatever!" (He really doesn't mean it—he wants your approval and wants to please you, but his hormones are driving him wacky and he just can't deal with them right now. So he yells at the one he's closest to and trusts the most. Lucky you.) Five minutes later,

---

The Great Secrets of Adolescence

- Your son thinks he's a klutz . . . and he is.
- Your son thinks he's dumb . . . and he does dumb things.
- Your son thinks he's ugly . . . and he is a little awkward looking.
- Your son really doesn't like himself . . . but he loves you.

---

he's saying, "Hey, Mom, do you know where I put my . . . ?" or "Mom, can you help me with . . . ?"

You see, all that work you've done in his earlier years really hasn't gone out the window. It's just hiding somewhere, waiting until he gets to be 22 years old, and you go from dumb to awfully smart again overnight. Then he'll be asking you for lots of advice.

If you've established a good relationship with your son through the early years, there's no reason to fear it will go south. Yes, it'll be a wavy line for a while, but it'll straighten out down the road as he learns to control his hormones.

Glued to the Mirror: The Adolescent Years

As your son enters those adolescent years, friends will become much more important. He'll spend more time grooming himself. He'll experiment with a new hairstyle, different types of clothes. He might want a tattoo. What's he doing? Your son is inventing his image, and he's trying on a lot of different identities. No one identity usually lasts that long (ah, I heard your sigh of relief), so don't worry. The time to be concerned is if your son becomes secretive in his actions and begins to withdraw from you and family activities. That's when you begin investigating.

Your son's body will be changing continually during this time—pimples will pop out, his voice will crack. He's never been interested in girls before, but now they loom large on his masculine landscape. He also studies the handsome, muscled guys on magazine covers and on TV, then takes a peek in the mirror at himself. He looks nothing like them, and that makes him feel inferior. Your son needs you to empathize with him but also to gently put things in perspective. Telling stories about embarrassing things you did during your own growing-up years provides shared laughter and a longer-term perspective for your son.

Yes, peers will be important. But emphasize that your son needs to have respect for everyone, not just the kids in his group. He also needs to respect you, his dad, and his siblings. A sassy mouth should not be tolerated.

> *Telling stories about embarrassing things you did during your own growing-up years provides shared laughter and a longer-term perspective for your son.*

If You Haven't Already Started an Allowance, Do So

"I can't afford to give my kid an allowance," you're saying. "We live on a shoestring budget."

But you can't afford *not* to give your son an allowance. How much money are you spending right now on his school clothes? His lunches? His sports uniforms? Add it all up and you'll be shocked at what you're actually spending.

It's important that your son learn how to budget his own money. Add up all the money you spend on your child during the year—groceries, doctor bills, and other such things aside—then divide it by 12. At the beginning of each month, give your child that amount. (When a child is younger, you'll want to do it weekly and use a smaller amount.) Explain that the allowance has to cover certain items (initially making him a list of those items will help) and that it has to last the month. No other money will be given to him until the beginning of the next month.

I guarantee your son will look at the money in that envelope and his first thought will be, *Hey, I'm rich! Look at all this money. I'm going to do this and this and this . . .*

Before long your son is out of money, and it's only the twelfth of the month. There's a lot of the month left. When he comes to you and says, "Uh, Mom, I wanted to do pizza at lunch on Tuesday, but I don't have any money," what do you say? "Well, payday is two weeks from Saturday, and that's when you'll get your allowance again." Now that's a teachable moment your son will remember. The next month he'll be a lot more careful about how he spends that money.

Don't Back Down on the Crucial Issues

It's a scary world out there, and your son needs to be informed. He doesn't need to hear "the facts" about drugs, sex, etc., from his buddies; he needs to hear them from you. The adolescent years are an important time to have this kind of a conversation with your son:

"Son, we need to talk about something really important. Drugs."

"Oh, Mom, I know all about drugs." He rolls his eyes.

"No," you say firmly. "I want you to listen. The day is coming really soon when someone is going to say to you, 'Hey, be cool like us. Drink this. Snort this.' I want you to know that I believe in you and that you're going to have the willpower and the guts to say no to people who are destroying their own lives and want to destroy yours."

When do you have this type of conversation? Preferably when your son is in sixth grade. Is it likely that someone will ask him to snort cocaine at 12 years old? No. But give it three years, and cocaine, heroin, and all sorts of pills can pop up right under his nose.

You can't put your son in a bubble, but you can plant a seed in his mind. That way when he's approached (and he will be), he'll connect the dots and remember what good ol' Mom used to say. And at that point, guess who ends up looking smart?

So talk with your son about things like drugs, drinking, and sex. (For more on sex, see chapter 8). Your son isn't a baby anymore, so don't baby him. But make your expectations clear: "I expect you under no circumstances to ever do drugs. Never to smoke weed. And not to drink beer or anything else alcoholic. You don't need to be like anybody else in that school. You're one of a kind. You're my son. Don't let anyone mess with you."

Another crucial issue is driving. You need to have this kind of discussion with your adolescent now, to set the tone before he even gets into high school:

"As you grow older, you can look forward to driving the family car. You're responsible at home and at school. You're doing life well. The proof is in the grades you bring home and in the way I see you helping your little sister. Being a member of our family means that you ought to reap the benefits. One of those benefits is driving the family car.

"I know you're only 12 right now, but the next four years are going to fly by. I want you to know that I believe in you and I trust you. However, if you decide not to be responsible

> ### Top 3 Survival Tips for Moms of Teens
>
> - Realize that clothing doesn't ultimately make the man (or woman).
> - Say "This too shall pass, this too shall pass" like a mantra until your heart rate slows down.
> - Laugh—wildly and long. (It really helps your stress level, and if your son thinks Mom's lost it, he might take it easy on you for the night.)

at home or school, you will not be driving the car. It's an open-and-shut case. As a parent, I'm not going to risk what your dad and I have financially by putting our car keys in the hands of someone who's not responsible. It's a huge responsibility to get behind the wheel of a car. Do we have to have a conversation about texting, or do you even need to hear what I'm going to tell you? Do we have to talk about not having five kids in the car with you, or do you already know that? I think we can discuss the rest later, but you get my drift."

What are you doing, Mom? You're coming alongside your adolescent and looking forward in life. You're painting a picture that life is great, and with it come some bonuses. But along with those bonuses come accountability and responsibility.

The Tumultuous Teenage Years (Ninth through Twelfth Grades)

Your teen has just entered those very critical years where he'll be tempted by more things than you can imagine—including drugs, alcohol, and sexual experiences. I don't have to tell you about them because you're right in the middle of them, and those worries are what keep you up all night. Yes, the risks during these years are great, but if you've set your foundation well with your child and taught him the ABCs of attitude, behavior, and character, and you've made sure that he always has the other ABCs in your home (acceptance, belonging, and competence), you have nothing to worry about. You may not always like your child during these years—let me assure you that your son won't always like you either—but both of you will get through them and come out on the other side. It'll take a lot of patience on both your parts.

Here's a short little guide to help you get through these years with less sweat and a sense of humor.

Be Aware of the World Your Son Lives in Every Day

Read the newspaper, check out online stories, and be aware of things that happen at your child's school. In other words, tune in to your son's world. It's not the same world you grew up in—it's far more *Use phrases like "Tell me more about that" to prompt conversation.* dangerous and growing more so every day. The most important thing is to tune in to your son's heart. He needs to know you care about him and his world. You may not like the beat of the music he's listening to, but listen to the lyrics. Use phrases like "Tell me more about that" to prompt conversation. Don't ever, ever interrogate him. That'll only shut him down. But show interest in what he's interested in, like building an eight-foot jet or playing Call of Duty 3 (even if you don't have a clue about computer games), and he'll respond.

Make Home a Safe Place

Home needs to be the place where your son can relax and be himself, even if he's grumpy. He shouldn't have to be who he's not when he's there. He needs to feel your unconditional love.

Keep an Eye on His Behavior

Hormone changes will cause wild mood swings, so expect moodiness. Expect your son to just grunt if you ask about his day and to disappear into his room until dinner. But if you notice your son spending all his time on the computer and jumping or looking nervous when you come in the room, you better check the computer's history. Also, if your son starts not caring about how he looks or not eating, remember that those aren't typical teenage behaviors. Be aware that some teens can sink into depression and may need your help or some professional help digging themselves out.

Find Ways to Get to Know His Friends

Make your home a place where your son and his friends can hang out. Converting a basement by adding comfy furniture will be a good draw (garage-sale furniture will do nicely, since it'll get pop spills and brownie stains). Provide food and for sure you'll have a group flocking to your house. Look at it this way: wouldn't you rather have a little (or a big) mess at your house and know what your son and his friends are up to rather than having them be at some other location—perhaps unsupervised? What you spend on snack food is a small thing compared to the relief you'll feel knowing your son is safe while he's exploring the world of friendships.

Make it a point to meet your son's friends. Usually that means attending a lot of school functions to see who he's hanging out with. But do it subtly. No teenager wants his mom to interrogate his friends or to hang around his friend group for very long. That would be embarrassing.

Set the Boundaries and Stick to Them

Family meetings, in which all members have a say in family outings, rules, and guidelines, are critical during this time. If you decide that your son has to be home by 10 p.m. on a Friday night and he blows it, he loses his privilege to go out for a while. Without boundaries, there is chaos, and you'll all experience the fallout.

Look for the Rewards

Catch your teen doing something wonderful. Slip him a commercial. "I loved seeing you help the librarian dig her car out of the snow. That was really kind of you. You didn't have to stop, yet you did."

Remember that your little-boy-turned-big-boy wants your approval the most. Though on the outside he may look grown-up and like he's not paying any attention to you, on the inside he's

> *Catch your teen doing something wonderful.*

still your little boy who's jumping up and down and saying, "Mom, look at me, look at me! See what I did? Aren't you proud of me?"

And when you get that infrequent hug and the "I love you, Mom," cherish it. It may be a long time until you hear it again. But you can be assured he's thinking it when you least expect it.

The MESS!

These years are messy years. "Think of what you see on the outside as what is happening on the inside" was some advice a friend once gave me. It really helps! So much is going on in your son's brain that it's just a little addled these days. And the result shows in his jumbled chaos of a room, in the way he leaves his dirty socks on the living room floor, and in the carnage from his after-school snacks that litter the kitchen.

Does this mean you shouldn't interrupt him to clean up the mess? Certainly not. In my house, whoever makes a mess is welcome to make it, as long as they clean it up. That's the Leman rule. Realize, though, that your standards are not your son's standards. But will it matter in 10 years how messy his room is? Or will it matter more that your 15-year-old son plops down on the couch and wants to talk with you about something that's bugging him?

Keep your eye on his heart.

Now that's perspective.

So keep your critical eye to a minimum. You may not like his spiked green hair or his style of clothing, but as long as he's decently covered, this too shall pass. Instead, keep your eye on his heart, for that's what will matter in the long run.

Driving the Car—a Privilege

Is there a law that says your teenager has to drive? No. This is a critical issue that you can't afford to take lightly. I've seen teenage sons dis their moms, even cuss them out, and you know what Mom does? Hands the car keys over to him as soon as he's done! What's wrong with that picture? Everything!

Driving the car is a privilege that your son will have once he gets his license. However, you hold the aces. That privilege is based on his being a respectful member of your family. If he chooses not to be, then he loses his family privilege of driving the car. Again, it's reality discipline: "B doesn't happen until A is completed."

Withhold the car keys from him once and it'll tick him off. He might go into a tirade. If he does, walk away into a different room, car keys in hand. Ignore him. When he sees you're not relenting, he'll try his best to change his tune. "Oh, come on, Mom. You know I didn't mean that."

Your response? Ignore him and go on with what you're doing.

Don't give in, Mom. Your son is testing you to see how much he can push your buttons. If you let him get away with that, he'll be pushing them in multiple areas as he grows up. But if he learns that what his mom says is what she means, that's a whole different ball game that can change his whole attitude and the respect level in your house.

Remember, You Hold the Aces

The other day, I talked with a mom who was concerned about her 16-year-old son. "He's starting to get into trouble, Dr. Leman. But he's driving now. He has friends and freedom. Just what the heck can I do? I can't put him in a time-out like I did when he was a little kid."

Don't sell yourself short, Mom. You still hold all the aces in your son's deck. He might be six-foot-one, but you're still the authority. The reality is, he can't be on the tennis team, run track, or play football without your signature. He can't even drive the car without your approval. The very same principles of reality discipline that work with little children (refer back to chapter 5 if you need a refresher) work even better with your older son because you have a lot more things in your arsenal to discipline him with: driving the car, playing sports, going out with the guys, having an allowance. Add to that the peer pressure of not wanting to be embarrassed in front of friends

---

What This Mom Did Right

My momma never put up with my lip or any of my shenanigans. No way, no how. When I was 13, I thought I was big stuff. I started smoking out behind the back of the school. I was dumb enough to think Momma wouldn't know the difference. One whiff and she was all over me.

"What are you doin', boy? Smokin'?" she asked.

I denied it and laughed behind her back.

It only took one dinner to set me straight. Dinner was late that night because my momma had an errand to run. You know what she served me for dinner? A whole plate of cigarettes. She didn't say a thing, just passed everybody else their dinner plates full of meat loaf and mashed potatoes (my favorite), and me my cigarette-filled plate.

I got the message . . . and flushed the cigarette I'd hidden in my pocket down the john later.

Twenty years later, she and I still talk about that event. But you know what? I never tried smoking again.

Jerome, New Jersey

---

or kept back from doing something with them (and then having to explain it), and reality discipline is powerful indeed.

The only thing you have to do is be consistent. Do what you say you'll do. Don't back down, even if he begs. Once the lesson is learned, your son won't be so "mommy deaf." He won't want to be embarrassed in front of his friends again either. And you won't have to become the perennial nag, a behavior that ticks him off and wears you out.

Get Your Son's Focus off Himself

The teen years are very self-centered years where your son will be thinking intensely about himself. *How do I fit in at school? With my friends? Do I look lame to girls?* His mind is littered with thoughts of "me, me, me." He's constantly comparing himself to other males to see if he's good enough and also competing to see if he can get the girl.

In these years of "me," why not do something others-centered together as a family activity to help get your son's perspective off himself and onto those who aren't as fortunate as he is?

For the past two years, the Terza family—mom, dad, and two teenage boys—has been going every Saturday to serve breakfast in a soup kitchen in a nearby city. It means getting up at 5:00 in the morning and having Dunkin' Donuts and coffee in the car in order to get to the center in time to cook eggs, pancakes, or whatever the kitchen is going to serve for breakfast.

Andy, who has just turned 16, told me, "The first time we did it, I couldn't believe my folks had signed my brother and me up for something so lame. I was ticked at having to get up early, and even worse, on a Saturday. I was in a bad mood the whole time I was in charge of cooking scrambled eggs. But then I got to serve the people who stood in the lines. Wow. That humbled me. I really saw how good I had it in life and how bad my attitude was." That day for Andy and his brother, Keith, was a real attitude check. Now it's a joy for the whole family to go. "It's made us all a lot more grateful for what we have, and more thoughtful toward others who don't have hardly anything in life," Andy says.

It comes to this: if you want to raise a son who is compassionate and others-centered, give him something to be compassionate about. There are lots of opportunities to help; just look for them.

Developing a heart of compassion for others will reap benefits for your son—and for all whose lives he touches—for the rest of his life.

What You Can Do

- Tell it like it is.
- Don't turn molehills into mountains.
- Stick to your guns.
- Don't take his hormones personally.

Nothin' New under the Son

Parents have been rearing adolescents for centuries. You're not the only mom to go through this wild ride. You don't have to reinvent the wheel. Sande and I have co-captained our Good Ship Family with five hands on deck and have navigated the waters successfully. You can too. It might not always be a ride you're thrilled about. But you need to remain calm, even when the waves are starting to wash over the boat.

Your son will take his emotional cues from you. He'll be watching how you handle the curveballs he (and life!) throws at you. You, Mom, set the emotional thermostat in your home. If you keep it a comfortable 72 degrees, chances are you'll all be okay. If you get too hot or cold about everything that happens during these years, everyone will suffer.

So stay calm. There's already enough heat from your son's hormones during these years to ratchet up the temperature in your house. Let the little stuff go and focus on the crucial issues. The blue hair and nose ring will disappear about the time your son goes to his first job interview anyway (unless he's working for a video store). Keeping that temperature in your home consistent will work best for all of you for the long haul.

But then again, I hear Fiji's really nice this time of year.

——— 8 ———

Guess What His Favorite Body Part Is

*There's no escaping our sex-laden world or a
boy's growing interest in sex. But how you respond to and address your son's sexuality can
make all the difference in his perspective.*

My daughter Krissy was giving a bath to both of her
children—Conner, three and a half, and Adeline,
one—when Conner noticed that something was different
about his sister. He looked closer, then exclaimed, "Mommy!
Is Adeline's penis broken?"

Boys are naturally drawn to the physical. They like to
look and touch. They're wired differently than girls, and for
good reason.

If your son is an adolescent, you'd be amazed at how many
of the finest body parts God ever created he's looked at today.

161

If you drive him to school or he takes the bus, chances are he's bombarded with everything from sexy girls on billboards selling Coke and Levis, to the girls who wear tight sweaters and short skirts who sit right next to him in calculus class. Then if he comes home and flips on the TV, what does he see? More voluptuous female figures. Even his computer games feature larger-than-average Barbie-busted women. So how can your son not look? Those beautiful female body parts are all around him!

Boys are naturally drawn to the physical. They like to look and touch.

However, the attitude your son will have about his sexuality and his resulting behavior has everything to do with how comfortable you are with him being male.

And it starts from the time he's a little kid.

It's a Natural Thing

In the early years, up until children go to school, they say exactly what they think. To them, exploring their sexuality is a natural part of life, and they have no problem telling you what they think or asking questions. They haven't been taught that it's dumb or wrong to ask questions about any subject, and to them, sex is just another subject of curiosity.

One of my favorite bath stories (other than the one about Conner and Adeline) is about the four-year-old who was happily taking a bath and making all the typical boy noises and splashes. All of a sudden he looked up at his mom and said, "Mommy, I love my penis."

His mom didn't quite know what to say, so she proceeded to name all his body parts and talk about how wonderful they were. "God gave us a great body, didn't he? A nose, two eyes, ears that can hear just about anything . . ." She went on and on in her explanation.

When she finally wound down her discourse and stopped, her son said, "Mom, I know that, but I still love my penis the best."

Sex education is an ongoing process. From the time your child first begins to speak and explore, he is taking in visual stimuli and trying to make sense of his body.

There will be plenty of opportunities for you to naturally explain the basics of sex to your son as he's growing up.

"Mommy, I love my penis."

Let's say you're driving in the car and you go up then down a hill, and your little boy says to you, "Mommy, that makes my thing feel funny. It feels good." Young kids will get sexual sensations like that. They'll climb a rope or do something else physical where another object comes in contact with their genital area. In their naïveté (at this point in life, children don't connect sexual feelings with sexual thoughts), they'll just announce, "Boy oh boy, that feels good."

Mom, you have a golden opportunity to say something like, "Isn't it wonderful how God has created our bodies to feel good? And there are certain parts of our bodies that really feel good to touch, don't they?" But if you freeze up and show embarrassment or say something like, "Son, that's not nice. We don't talk about things like that," what message have you sent your son? *Wait a minute, you better not talk about that. That's nasty and dirty.*

So what does that make your son think? *Hey, I better keep that secret and explore it in private where nobody else can see.*

Boys who feel they have to explore their sexuality in private are much more likely to become interested in pornographic images because they are primed to hide their interest in sex. So why not do your boy a favor and talk about it openly?

Your son is also naturally noticing things about how pets and other animals relate. Like the day five-year-old Jason was at a horse farm and saw the stallion's "winkie," as he called it, hanging out. "Hey, Mom!" he yelled across the stable at the top of his voice. "Look! That horse has a winkie too, just like mine!"

Boys who feel they have to explore their sexuality in private are much more likely to become interested in pornographic images because they are primed to hide their interest in sex.

Another time, about six months later, Jason saw that same frisky stallion trying to mount a mare. "Hey, Mom!" he yelled again (this boy didn't do anything quietly). "Look! That boy horse is wrestling the girl horse. What's he doing?"

After that, Jason's mom thought it might be time to explain a little bit about the birds and the bees, so she explained that boys have penises and girls have vaginas. And a boy has to put his penis in a girl's vagina in order to make a baby. So that's what the horse was trying to do—make a baby.

Jason listened intently, then sighed. "Well, that sure seems like a lot of work for the boy horse. I bet he gets tired."

The mom was glad nobody else overheard *that* conversation.

In the early years, the best thing you can do as a parent is to answer the questions children ask in a calm, straightforward manner. Don't go beyond what your son asks. If he wants more information, he'll ask you. If not, he'll be satisfied with the explanation you've already given.

Do Babies Come from Eggs?

As soon as your son goes to school, he'll hear a lot of information about love and sex here and there from his peers, such as:

> "Babies come from eggs, just like chickens. But it takes longer to hatch them."
>
> "When a daddy kisses a mommy, she has a baby."
>
> "When a mommy goes to the hospital to have a baby, they open a door in her tummy and the baby crawls out."

As he gets older, he'll get even more information, especially when he hits fourth grade. That's usually the time when schools play the movie about the birds and the bees, and children think it's silly and giggle. Then in fifth grade, many schools have children raise chicks from the egg on and talk about the cycle of birth and life. Afterward, when the chicks hatch, the boys and girls go to a separate class to learn about what makes girls girls and what makes boys boys, and how the physical act of sex takes place.

But the wise parent will prepare their child along the way by answering questions as they come up and by looking for opportunities to explain what they believe about sex. Remember what I said about sex education being an ongoing process? If you reduce it to "the talk," you're sadly missing the point. Why be embarrassed to talk with your child about what is natural?

My suggestion is that if by the age of nine your child hasn't asked where babies come from, you spark the conversation. You might be wise to start off the subject when you're in the car on the interstate—or at least some place with no red lights or stop signs, so your nine-year-old won't go flying out of the car. Sometimes talking about difficult subjects is easier if it's not eyeball to eyeball.

One Day in the Life of a Mom

I'm a mom with three boys. Since we seemed to have a lot of discussions about their penises (a body part they were tremendously interested in), I decided that we'd just call that body part "Mr. Wiggles." That way, if anyone was overhearing our conversations, which took place even at the supermarket and the hair salon, it wouldn't be as embarrassing.

One day I was at the mall with my youngest son, who was two at the time, trying to find some new shoes for him. He was tremendously scroochy, couldn't seem to focus on anything, and was constantly lagging behind me. Finally I stopped in the middle of the aisle at the mall and said, "Jared, will you please get the wiggles out?"

He looked at me, shrugged, and said, "Okay, Mom."

I took a few more steps but could tell he still wasn't following me. So I looked back in frustration.

He'd gotten the wiggles out all right. *Mr. Wiggles.* There was my son, standing in the middle of the mall with his pants unzipped, holding Mr. Wiggles for all to see!

Needless to say, that family story will go down in history.

And no, we didn't get shoes that day. Let's just say we made a fast exit from the mall. . . .

Brenda, Tennessee

A simple explanation will do. Explain the basic male and female body parts—that a daddy has a penis and a mommy has a vagina. The daddy has to put his penis inside the mommy to release his sperm, which will travel up into that mommy to meet with her egg. When a sperm meets an egg, it fertilizes the egg, and that's how a baby starts forming.

Your son will most likely be quiet as he processes all these candid facts of life. Then you'll probably hear, "You mean you and Daddy did that?"

You nod.

Another thought from the backseat: "And you did it *two* times, to get me and my sister?"

You nod again.

"That's so gross!"

There are a lot of little pamphlets, books, and CDs about how to explain the "facts of life," but they can never replace hearing the facts from you. After all, no one knows your child better than you.

But what *you* think about sex is crucial to how you'll present it to your child.

"You mean you and Daddy did that?"

What Do You Think about Sex?

No new parent thinks, *Yippee! I can't wait until I can talk to my kid about sex.* For most parents, even the concept receives a groan. Most parents aren't comfortable talking about sex, which always hits me as strange, since if you're doing it, why not talk about it? Many parents worry that by bringing up the subject, they'll thrust their children into sexual exploration. Actually, the opposite is true.

If your kids aren't getting the answers from you, who will they get them from? Their peers, who will give them a boatload of misinformation? From other adults or textbooks that may not have the perspective on sex that you want your child to hear? From society, which will give them conflicting messages about what sex and love are, what's appropriate, and what's not?

Talking about sex is a tough job, but somebody's got to do it. We're all sexual beings from day one, and kids have questions along the way. The more straightforwardly you can answer them, the better.

Some parents are hindered in talking about sex because it was considered something dirty in their home as they grew up. No one talked about it because it wasn't acceptable. This happens often in more religiously conservative homes (which is sad, since God almighty himself created sex!), and it can lead to low self-esteem and the inability to enjoy sex in marriage.

If you struggle with talking about sex with your children, it's most likely for one of several reasons.

Your mom and dad didn't talk about it. Maybe you just figured sex out yourself, and you hope your children do too! Or you fear saying "the wrong thing." But do you really want your son to struggle through figuring it out for himself? The stakes today, with all the sexual diseases, are even higher than they were when you were growing up. Why not set an example for the next generation?

You're not sure what to say or how to word it. If you're ignorant, read several of the pamphlets on explaining the birds and the bees and come up with your own angle that will make sense to your son.

You're embarrassed about your own body. Some of you grew up in a family where no one talked about the body— especially the penis and the vagina. The subject was taboo. The genital area was referred to as "down there." If that is your background, gather the information you need and then gather your courage. Call a spade a spade. Be straightforward as you talk to your children. They deserve to hear the facts from you.

You made sexual mistakes yourself. Because you messed up, you think you're not the one who should talk to your kids about what they should do or shouldn't do. But you're dead wrong. You're *exactly* the person who should talk to them because you know the consequences of not treating sex the way God almighty intended—only within the marriage relationship. You don't have to explain to your kids blow by blow what you did. But they need to know that you have regrets and that you don't want them to have those same

What This Mom Did Right

I love my mom for calling things like they are. But maybe with all boys in the house, she didn't have the opportunity to do otherwise. She was one gutsy woman. When I turned 10, she sat me down for "the talk." We went through the drive-through at A&W and got root beer floats, then sat in the car. It was raining, so I had nowhere else to go once she started in on the surprise topic. Man, that stunk. But she was smart to do it that way.

My mom didn't pull any punches. What I remember most is her talk about girls. I thought I knew it all, but I was as clueless as they come. I still remember her advice . . . even if I was a little embarrassed at the time.

Mac, Tennessee

regrets, which is why you're talking to them now. That ought to make them perk up their ears and listen.

Above all, you need to set the context: sex is a wonderful experience that bonds two people together for a lifetime, and this bond should form only within the safety and security of marriage. When it occurs outside of that safe bond of marriage, all kinds of regrets can occur to cause harm to both the man and the woman. And sometimes children are born out of wedlock, without the safety and security of living in a home with both Mom and Dad present and actively involved in their lives.

Uh-Oh, I Think I Saw a Hair under His Arm . . .

It's that time—that wonderful time of life called *adolescence*, when your son's voice is starting to change. You think you see a hair under his arm, and you've caught him holding or rubbing his penis a time or two . . . and he's not even aware of it. So what do you do now?

You panic. *I haven't a clue what to do, what to say.*

169

It's your time to step up to the plate. Remember what we talked about earlier—that the most important relationships in a family are the opposite-sex ones? Don't leave the important information on sex up to your husband, your ex, or whatever men are in your life. And the postman sure isn't going to help out. Mom, who better than you to tell your son how a girl wants to be treated? About the changes in a girl's body? How being around a boy makes a girl feel? About how a girl wants to be touched, and why it's important to be careful where you touch a girl?

> *Mom, who better than you to tell your son how a girl wants to be treated?*

The ideal is for both Mom and Dad to be present to talk with their son about sex. But if you're a single parent, you may not have that option. If you don't, remember that the most important conversation your son can have is with you.

(And for daughters, conversely, it's the dad who should explain how boys develop, think, and respond when they like girls.)

During early puberty (sixth and seventh grade), your son is spending a lot of time and attention on things about himself from the neck up—those zits that pop up out of nowhere, bad hair days, and a voice that cracks at embarrassing times. It's the perfect time to begin opening the doors of conversation to what a lot of kids call "first base"—what will happen from the neck up on dates. Starting with a more relatable and less embarrassing issue will help you both open up to each other and grow more comfortable instead of trying to tackle all the issues "below the belt" at the same time.

The best thing you can do as a mom during this transition in your child's life is to show empathy over those first pimples and get some over-the-counter medication to help. Take your son to a real hairstylist (not just a barber) to get a hairstyle that works for him with minimal care. Make a trip together to Walgreens to pick out deodorant if your son needs it.

By sixth grade, your son should have a handle on these basic hygiene skills, because his hormones will be fully in the "on" position. All of a sudden he might become more concerned about the label of the clothes he's wearing (which he never gave a rip about before).

By seventh and eighth grade, your son is moving into his adolescent years, where he'll be dominated by hormones. During football games on TV, you'll notice his eyes straying to the cheerleaders and their short skirts. All this is very normal behavior for a teenage boy.

But I'll be blunt. Your son is entering a turbulent world. In today's society, it's common behavior for teen boys to engage in fondling breasts, oral sex (which many teens don't even think of as sex), and sexual intercourse. With high statistics on out-of-wedlock pregnancies, STDs, and broken hearts, your son is entering what I call a critical time of life. By that, I mean that one sexual experience can give your son a disease he'll have to deal with for a lifetime (or that will shorten his lifetime). With so much at stake, it's crucial that your son have as much information as possible about his sexuality, how his body works, and why his actions now can change his life.

What's a Wet Dream?

If you want to see your husband choke on his morning cantaloupe, ask him out of the blue, "Honey, what was your first wet dream like?" There's not a man on this earth who can't tell you what his first wet dream was like. That's because the

171

experience takes every young man by tremendous surprise and is therefore memorable.

There's something you have to know about boys. God created your son in such a way that when he starts to mature and his body goes through changes, he's going to have nocturnal emissions. That's a big term for what many people call *wet dreams*. A wet dream is a sexual dream that young men in particular have, and many times they'll actually ejaculate in their underwear. When they wake up from the dream, they'll think, *Whoa! What was all that about?* But it's actually a very natural thing. Nothing dirty or embarrassing about it at all.

So wash your son's sheets when he has a wet dream without making any big deal about it. Talk with your son about what just happened. Explain that wet dreams are a sign that your boy is indeed growing up. They're also a sign that he is now able sexually to create life. "That ability comes with some real responsibilities," you need to tell him. "You need to be very, very careful what you do with Mr. Happy down there. He belongs in *your* pants, not someone else's."

> *"You need to be very, very careful what you do with Mr. Happy down there. He belongs in your pants, not someone else's."*

Again, the stakes are too high *not* to have this discussion. Too many girls have become pregnant at 13 or 15 years of age. It happens all the time. But what a tough situation that sets up for the girl—and for the child. Most of the time, the guy walks away and leaves the girl with the consequences.

Take Travis Henry, a former NFL running back, for example. According to a 2009 *New York Times* article, this 33-year-old athlete, "who played for three teams from 2001 to 2007, has nine children—each by a different mother, some born as closely as a few months apart."[1]

Henry grew up with nothing but became a gifted athlete who was paid a lot of money just to play football. But what did he do with his chance? He screwed his life up (no pun intended). And the saddest thing of all is that his poor decisions impacted nine different women and nine little children. And now, at the time of this writing, he has eleven children.

That's why it's important that Mr. Happy stays where he belongs.

It's a Fact of Life

It's not a question of whether your son will masturbate, but a fact: your son *will* masturbate (and if you have a daughter, she very likely will too). He'll do it mostly in his bedroom, in the bathroom, in the shower, or behind another locked door. We all need privacy, and so does your son as he's grappling with all the tremendous hormonal urges that now surge through his body. You as a parent need to make sure there's a lock on his door. In fact, make a big deal out of it: "Honey, you're getting older. We need to ensure that you have some privacy. You need to get a lock on your door."

In the adolescent years, your son's body is beginning to produce semen at a very high rate, and there are only three ways that semen can come out: through nocturnal emission, masturbation, or sexual intercourse. You can help your son choose how to handle this natural biological pressure by talking with him about it as a natural thing, instead of making it a secretive behavior that he has to hide.

Nocturnal emission will just happen; it's not something that your son can control since it occurs when he's sleeping.

Ask Dr. Leman

I'm in shock. I just found a porn magazine underneath my 13-year-old son's bed. What do I do?

Desperate in Milwaukee

Dear Desperate:

Here's my suggestion. Take that magazine, put it on the coffee table next to your other magazines like *Good Housekeeping*, and let your son discover it for himself. When he gets that green look on his face, you'll know he's spotted it.

Then say casually, "Honey, I found this in the strangest place today— under your bed. I'm glad to see you have a natural interest in the opposite sex, but let's talk about this magazine for just a minute. Do you think it's a positive portrayal of who women are, or a negative one? Is it respectful or disrespectful?"

The important thing is not to shame the kid. Encourage his natural tendency to check out the opposite sex, but point to what's wrong with the magazine. "Frankly, I find this magazine demeaning to me or to any other woman. And I don't want to have such a magazine in my home."

What are you doing? You're throwing up the orange flag and saying, "That's a foul. Not something we're going to do in our home."

Who should get rid of the magazine? Not you. You didn't buy it, did you? Let your son dispose of it. It's his responsibility. Don't own what isn't yours.

Dr. Leman

Masturbation is a way for him to release the pressure that builds up as he matures.

The alternative—sexual intercourse—is one you need to encourage your son *not* to pursue until he's walked down that aisle of wedded bliss.

A Natural Curiosity

As your son matures, he will have a very natural curiosity about the female body and how it works. A beautiful girl will walk by, and his Mr. Happy will want to do a happy dance. But you can help your son pursue his interest in a way that is helpful rather than harmful. Get books that explain how a female's body works and that talk about sex and can answer his questions. Talk with him about all his body's changes and the changes that are going on in a girl's body.

If you don't answer his questions or help him find answers, your son will be visually stimulated other ways—like late-night TV that has explicit programming, pornographic magazines, or internet porn. Wouldn't you rather be the one providing the info? And by the way, since you are the purveyor of information to your son, make sure he understands that no woman likes to be grabbed. Ever.

That First Date

Your son is ready to go on his first date, and you're more nervous than he is. Will he follow the boundaries that you've set up for sexual activity? And what about the girl? What about peer pressure?

Before any date occurs, it's critical that you talk with your son about how to treat girls. The old commandment is true: treat others as you'd want to be treated. Teach your son how to make conversation with girls. Teach him that our bodies are wonderfully created and that sex is an amazing experience, but that a great reward waits for those who save sexual activity for marriage. Then there are no regrets, no pieces of yourself left behind.

Set boundaries for what can happen on a first date. Remind your son that a kiss is something special to be shared, not just "what you have to do" at the end of a date. A hand squeeze, a smile, and a "Thanks, I had a good time" will do.

What You Can Do

- Teach your son naturally about sex, answering his questions as he grows up.
- Be aware of the changes in his body and treat them as normal, not something secretive to be hidden.
- Encourage his natural interest in girls by providing him straightforward information.
- Talk with him about the reasons for boundaries in his sexual behavior.

As things progress in your son's dating life (*if* they do—first relationships are often very fickle), talk about how proceeding to "first base" (which addresses body parts from the neck up), "second base" (from the neck to the waist), "third base" (from the waist down), and "home plate" (sexual intercourse) can change the dynamics of a relationship. Is he really ready to accept the responsibility that goes along with the progression?

Talk with your son about the different "bases" and what they mean before you ever allow him to go on a date. Even better, suggest that your son group date for a while (in other words, a bunch of guys go out with a bunch of girls to get to know them better) before he pursues single dating. It will save your son a lot of embarrassment and also stall his involvement with a girl until he has a little more experience with handling his raging hormones.

The Power of Positive Expectations

If you teach your son your moral values, how to handle the pressures of his sexuality, how to treat a girl on a date (with brotherly concern!), and to keep Mr. Happy in his pants, then trust him to do the right thing. Remember the power of positive expectations? Expect the best, and you'll get the best.

As your son grows into a man, he'll naturally think of sex at least 33 times a day. But it's what he does with those thoughts that counts.

— 9 —

Doormat, Dishrag,
or Strong and Smart?

*How do you treat yourself, Mom? And how do
the men in your life treat you? Now's the time to
stand up for yourself—for the sake of your son
and his future relationships.*

Do any of the following sound like you?

- I don't like it when people get upset with me.
- I want everyone to be happy.
- I go out of my way to please others.
- I find it hard to say no.
- I don't feel like I get much respect at home . . . or any-
  where else.
- Sometimes I get overwhelmed with everything I have
  to do.

179

- Deep down, I don't feel good enough.
- I just can't do enough.

If so, join a very populated club. The majority of moms feel just like you. Here you moms are, juggling feats day after day that would kill us men, and you still think you haven't done enough.

That's the way Hannah felt when she came to see me in my counseling office. Bright, talented, and intelligent, this working mom looked successful on the surface. But deep underneath, where it matters, she was always second-guessing herself. "Dr. Leman, I can never do enough in my day to make people happy. My son isn't happy, my husband isn't happy, and my boss isn't happy. And my mother? She isn't happy either. She keeps harping about me working too hard and telling me I need more rest. But how am I going to do that? I don't even have time to get done what I have to do now. So I keep running faster and faster to get things done, but it's never enough. I try to please others, but it's not working. I'm exhausted. And I'm feeling really depressed."

Not even three superwomen moving at lightning speed could get all that done. So how could she?

As I looked at the dark circles under Hannah's eyes, I agreed that something had to change. And the root of her trouble was showing itself clearly in what she'd just told me. Notice all the "I" in her speech:

- I can never do enough.
- How am I going to do that?
- I don't even have time to get done what I have to do now.

- I keep running faster.
- I try to please others.

When I listened to what Hannah attempted to accomplish during her day, I was stunned. Not even three superwomen moving at lightning speed could get all that done. So how could she? What she was asking of herself was impossible for any human being! Even more, with her uses of "I," she was taking the weight of all the responsibility on herself. It was her responsibility to make sure her husband's and son's shorts were clean. She was the one who always had to pick up the younger kids from day care, even though her husband was home before her. Her boss always seemed to dump extra projects on her, and she took them. And she was the one planning the Valentine's party for her son's third-grade class.

Why would a smart, competent woman like Hannah—and like yourself—take on so much?

I Only Count When . . .

It all has to do with your *personal lifestyle*—the way you look at yourself, others, and the world.

How would you complete the statement, "I only count when . . ."? Take a minute to think about it and jot down some notes. I'll wait. . . .

Got your answer? Take a careful look at it. Because within that answer is your life theme. It's the mantra you live by every moment. Here are some common mantras for women (I'll explain more later why they're less likely for men):

- I only count when I please others.
- I only count when I'm doing something.
- I only count when I'm doing something for others.

181

- I only count when everyone approves of what I do.
- I only count when I keep everything smooth and on an even keel.
- I only count when I'm doing everything I can possibly do.
- I only count when I put others first.
- I only count when everyone likes me.

Do any of those sound familiar?

Whatever your life theme or lifestyle is, you are living it every minute of the day. It directs what you do, what you say, and how you think and feel. But where did it come from?

Lifestyle is a term coined by Alfred Adler, an Austrian psychologist and the founder of individual psychology. He believed that from babyhood on, you started forming an individual life plan that caused you to pursue certain goals. Obviously, you didn't do this consciously (you were an infant!), but the information was all registered in your little brain.[1]

According to Rudolph Dreikurs, one of Alfred Adler's leading disciples, you as a growing child experienced both heredity *and* environment and drew your own conclusions. As you experienced your environment wherever you spent your childhood (your family, foster family, blended family, welfare institution), you discovered where you were skilled and strong and where you were weak and lacking in ability. As you sorted out all of those experiences with their pluses and minuses, your personality took shape.[2]

As you developed your lifestyle by pursuing your basic goal, you also developed your life theme—your personal mottos and slogans, the ideas that you now subconsciously repeat to yourself daily and believe with all your heart. That life theme always has to do with your self-image and your sense of self-worth. It's how you complete the statement, "I only count when . . ."

But are you really only what your life theme tells you? Or could it be lying to you? And how does this life theme make you treat yourself? Are you a doormat, a dishrag, or strong and smart? And what does how you treat yourself have to do with a book on mothers and sons?

I Just Want People to Be Happy

Are you spending your life trying to make people happy? Trying to make your husband happy? Your son? Your other children? Your boss? The head of the PTA? And it goes on and on and on. Let me be blunt. You can *never, ever* make everybody happy, and that's not your job.

But if you're wired to be a pleaser, trying to make people happy comes so naturally you don't even think about it . . . until the cost to yourself is too high and you're exhausted.

Pleasers are driven by the need to be liked by everyone. That's why the majority of pleasers are women just like you.

Why are they not men? (Well, I think in the continental United States, there are probably nine men who are pleasers, but I won't divulge where they live.) Men are wired to get a job done, and women are wired for relationships. Frankly, it doesn't matter as much to men in general if they're liked by others, but it certainly matters to women.

Pleasers are driven by the need to be liked by everyone.

Pleasers are often firstborn women who are driven to get it all done and have been primed for excellence since the minute they came out of their mother's womb, as well as secondborn or middleborn kids who just want the ocean waves of life to be smooth. The pleaser's mantras in life are things like:

Are You a Pleaser?

Do you:
- walk on eggshells to keep everybody happy, especially your family?
- agree with others just so you won't rock the boat?
- get little respect from your spouse or children?
- believe that what you do is more important than who you are?
- feel insecure, like you're not good enough?
- remember your father as a stern disciplinarian who always had to have things his way, rather than a loving, gentle daddy?
- feel like you can never do things right?
- want to run away from life's hassles because you're overwhelmed?

- Everybody's got to like me.
- I have to please other people.
- If other people are unhappy, it's my fault.

Pleasers try hard to gain everyone's approval—particularly their families'—and often at great cost to themselves. They typically have a poor self-image, which is why they have to do everything they can to keep everyone else happy. They believe the lie that they are valued for what they *do*, not for who they are.

Do you find yourself smiling and agreeing with people just so you won't rock the boat, when inwardly you're thinking, *No way! That's the dumbest thing I've ever heard!* Yet you don't have the courage to speak up and say what you really think? That's why you often find yourself pulled along by others' ideas and activities and feel overwhelmed.

Measuring Up

Do you ever feel like you can't quite measure up? Like everything you try to do isn't good enough, yet you're doing your best? That too is a trait of a pleaser. Pleasers are often perfectionists who constantly worry about being perfect. *If I'm not the perfect wife, perfect mother, perfect this-and-that, my world will come crashing in.*

So how did you get yourself on this high-jump bar of life?

It all started with how your daddy treated you. (Again, remember the importance of opposite-sex relationships.) Were you good enough for your daddy, or did you not measure up as you were growing up? It doesn't matter whether the disapproval was subtle or obvious, you felt it just the same. And if your mom was critical, you got hit with a double whammy of thinking you weren't good enough.

Because of the way you grew up, you will always have this life theme running through your mind: "I only count when . . ." But it doesn't have to hold you hostage. If you're aware that such a life theme is affecting your thoughts and actions, you can ask yourself, *Why am I acting this way? Why am I thinking so negatively about myself? Why do I have to do everything? Just because I'm trying to be perfect? To measure up?* Then your logic and reasoning can kick in. *But nobody can do all that, so why am I setting myself up to do what's impossible?*

Marianne had three young boys under the age of six. She was simply exhausted. She didn't have a minute of the day to herself in caring for her children, and they rarely slept at the same time. But her husband? When Frank got home, he insisted that his dinner be ready on schedule—5:30 on the dot. And he made his disapproval known by his glowering silence if it wasn't. And because he "worked all day to put food on the table" (as he always put it), he deserved to retreat to the den with the doors shut to watch his favorite cop thriller.

But you know what Frank really deserved—and needed? A swift kick in the keister for being such an arrogant, controlling jerk.

Did Marianne see that at first? No, she thought the problem was all with her. That she wasn't doing enough to make Frank happy. That the children were taking too much of her time, so he wasn't happy with her. And above all, she wanted Frank to be happy. After all, didn't he deserve to be happy? He was right. He did work hard all day, and she didn't make any money. He was a good provider for their family, so he did deserve to rest at night, didn't he?

> *You know what Frank really deserved—and needed? A swift kick in the keister for being such an arrogant, controlling jerk.*

Marianne's litany of degrading herself went on and on until I stopped it with a single question: "How does Frank's treatment of you make you feel?"

Then the tears began and the truth began pouring out. Marianne was a pleaser who had never been able to please her authoritarian father. He too had demanded dinner promptly within 10 minutes of his arrival home, and Marianne's mother always obediently served it. Even if she was already cooking something for dinner, she went out of her way to run to the grocery store in the afternoon if he called and demanded (not requested, *demanded*) something else. By watching her mother, Marianne had been primed to believe that that was how women were supposed to act with their husbands.

But she was wrong. Dead wrong. Yes, when you marry, you're making a commitment to please your husband. But

What This Mom Did Right

I'm a single mom, and I've dated a lot of guys in the last three years since my ex left. When I found Aaron, I thought he was a keeper. He was everything I wanted in a guy—strong, successful, charming.

After a couple months, I allowed my son to meet him, and Aaron started hanging around a lot more. He tried to be Kyle's buddy, but it only seemed to make Kyle mad. (He had just turned 12.) One day I was ticked off at Kyle for not trying to get along with Aaron, and Kyle blew up at me. "You don't even act like my mom anymore!" he yelled. "You act just like you used to when Dad was around!"

I was stunned. When I finally figured out what he was saying, I started to sob. Kyle was right. My ex used to abuse me and threatened to hit Kyle, so I always went out of my way to make sure everything was "just right" at home so he wouldn't get upset. I was doing the same thing with Aaron. Kyle was right. Man, am I dumb or what?

A week later I picked up your book *Pleasers* and read it cover to cover, twice. Thanks, I really needed that book. I understand myself so much better now—why I do what I do.

And you know what? I took your advice. I dumped the chump. I decided that, for a while, it's just going to be Kyle and me. Now we're getting along a lot better.

Felicia, New Jersey

he's also making a commitment to please you. It's a mutual thing, not a master-servant thing.

Yet because Marianne's mother chose to be a dishrag, bending to whatever her husband wanted, she instilled in her daughter the lie that women are to be subservient to men. And now her daughter was paying the price.

You see, pleasers often marry controllers.

What's a Controller?

Controllers have these life themes:

- I only count when people do what I say.

- I only count when I'm running the show.
- I only count when I'm in control of the situation.

Controllers are powerful people who want to control everything and everyone. Nothing escapes their critical, perfectionistic eye. No one they deal with is free from the strings they try to attach. Often they are firstborns who lived with high expectations from their parents and were expected to take care of their younger siblings. So they learned how to be in charge—and how to do it well. The problem is that their need to be in control grew into a well-formed lifestyle that is difficult to change.

Controllers are usually most comfortable with holding people at arm's length. They often avoid intimacy—unless it's on their own terms—because they fear losing control. Controllers are determined that no one is going to take control of them.

Controllers are powerful people who want to control everything and everyone.

Controllers also have a need to be right, and they seldom lose an argument. They're always trying to jump the high bar of life, and they insist that those around them clear it as well. They're fault-finders who put down and degrade others with subtle—or not-so-subtle—humor.

Here's the catch. You'd think that controllers would always be assertive, aggressive types. Indeed, they can be. But they can also be temperamental, insecure, shy, and quiet types who control by their brooding silence and disapproval. Some controllers shout and intimidate to get their way, others physically abuse, and still others make their families walk on eggshells around them.

Is Your Man a Controller?

Does he ...

- tend to be critical and find fault?
- hold himself and others to a high standard of excellence?
- put others down?
- have a bad relationship with his mother?
- always get his way?
- lose his temper frequently?
- prefer to run the show—no matter what the activity is?
- give you the silent treatment when he's not pleased with you?
- find it hard to say he was wrong and excuse himself instead?
- get physical—shoving you, hitting you or your kids, or smashing things?
- control the finances tightly?
- always have to win?

Why Controllers and Pleasers Marry

Have you ever heard "opposites attract"? That's why pleasers often marry controllers. When they're dating, the pleaser falls into the trap of enjoying the attention and the focus. "He's so in charge," the pleaser says. "I love strong men." And the attraction grows.

But what most pleasers don't realize up front is that the strength they think they see in that man is actually a hunger for power and control. When the relationship grows, the controller's true colors will be shown—he will indeed want to run things, and you won't be allowed a say. And if you complain? Well, there's something wrong with you. Never with him.

If you realize that you're married to a controller, it's important for you to know that you are not going to change

If you complain? Well, there's something wrong with you. Never with him.

189

your spouse. Controlling habits are deeply ingrained in him. (Now, if you're in a relationship with a controller and you aren't married yet, I have different advice: Run! Get away now!)

You can never change anyone else's behavior. You can change only your own behavior and your way of interacting.

Here's what I mean.

Angie had been married to a controller for 15 years. They had four children, two of them boys. She'd put up with a lot from her husband, Dave, over the years, including feeling like she was always a second-class citizen. But one Thursday night dinner changed everything for her.

Her oldest son, Matt, who was 13, just tipped his glass her direction to refill his Mountain Dew during dinner. He didn't ask, "Mom, would you please get me some more Mountain Dew?" or "Mom, would you mind if I pour myself some more Mountain Dew?" No, he just looked at her, tipped his glass at her like she was a servant, and expected her to hop up and get it.

Exactly what his father had done to her all their married life.

For Angie, the buck stopped right there. She got up from the table, got in the family minivan, and drove around for an hour while she formulated her plan. During that hour she decided that no longer would she be anyone's doormat. She was a person worthy of respect, and she didn't have to take it any longer.

Was it easy for Angie to make changes? No. Her own patterns of relating to her family were deeply ingrained. But she was determined that her sons not follow the same pattern as her husband. Over the next week, she slowly set up a schedule and assigned each of her boys some simple tasks such as clearing the table, putting the dishes in the dishwasher, and starting a load of laundry.

When her husband left his own Mountain Dew cans on the counter, she didn't touch them. She just let them stack up until they were falling on the floor. One day Dave said to her in disgust, "Look at this place. There are cans all over the counter. Go put these in the garage."

What did this pleaser-woman-turned-strong-and-smart do? Looked at her husband evenly and said calmly, "The recycle bin is to the left, right as you open the garage door." And then she continued doing what she was doing.

Her shocked husband was so stunned he didn't even know what to say. He stomped away into the den . . . but later she noticed that the pop cans had disappeared off the counter. And somehow they didn't show up there anymore.

It was a small victory, but a start.

And it all came as a result of Angie deciding that no longer would she be a doormat for her husband to walk on or a limp dishrag who always did his bid-

Your son is watching.

ding. She would be who God almighty created her to be: a woman worthy of respect.

Good for you, Angie.

I'll be blunt. Some of you have a man who is toxic to you—and to your son. So why are you putting up with him? You deserve better. You might think that having a man in the home is better than having no man at all. But think again. If the role model of masculinity your son sees is a man who has to control you and your kids through shouting, intimidation, or any other kind of abuse, you'd be better off without him.

Your son is watching. He's watching how you relate to your husband or your boyfriend. He's watching how your

191

husband or boyfriend treats you and how you respond to such treatment.

If you always do a controller's bidding, you're teaching your son that that's the way men should treat women—as second-class citizens who need to be controlled.

Mom, for your son's sake, you need to stand up for yourself. Don't allow yourself to be controlled. You won't change your man's tendency to be a controller. He needs to know clearly from you that if he wants to control himself, he's welcome to, but when he tries to control you and everyone else in the family, you won't put up with it.

(A very important note: If your controller has reached any level of verbal or physical abusiveness, run—don't walk—to the nearest competent professional therapist who can advise you. If the treatment has escalated, take your children with you and get away to a safe location.)

Because You're Worth It

You're not a doormat. You're not a dishrag. You're a strong and smart woman who accomplishes more things in an hour than a male can get done in a whole day. (Just watching how my wife can juggle everything makes me dizzy.) And you can even do more than one thing at a time! (A constant wonderment to us men.)

Never, ever allow yourself to be treated with anything other than respect in your own home.

You are a precious human being, created by God almighty himself. You may have some hang-ups to work through, especially if you lived through a difficult childhood. But never, ever allow yourself to be treated with anything other

What You Can Do

- Identify your life themes that have formed your lifestyle.
- Make a list of the pleasing tendencies you see in yourself.
- Ask yourself, *How do these pleasing tendencies affect the way I view myself? The way I act? The way I allow myself to be treated? What do I need to start doing differently?*

than respect in your own home—for your sake and your son's.

His eyes are always watching. And right now, his own lifestyle and life themes are being formed. So what will they be?

How you treat yourself and how you allow the men in your life to treat you will help form his views of who he is as a man, who women are, and how women should be treated. So treat yourself right and don't put up with any crap. If you can't do it for yourself, do it for your son.

10

On Duty or MIA?

Does your son have an actively involved father or an emotionally or physically MIA daddy? Here's what to do with each one.

A year ago, I did a survey in one of my "Mother Stress" seminars. I asked the group of women what the three top stressors in their life were. They all agreed on the same ones, and they even put them in the same order:

- Kids
- Lack of time
- Husband

Surprised? Bet you aren't. I bet you agreed with every single one of them when you thought through what causes you stress.

I know this is a book about *mothers* and sons. But I'd be remiss if I didn't talk about the other man in your life—your husband or your ex—because he has everything to do with your son and with you.

Take a look at those top stressors again. Now just who do you think could help you the most with all three? You got it! Your husband. (Exes? Well, they're not usually quite so helpful, but they can step up to the plate and help with the first two items on your stress list.)

Who better than your husband to help you do all you need to with the children? Who better to help get done what you can't get done even with superhuman strength? And who better to help address your third stressor but your husband himself?

> *Your husband wants to be your hero. He wants to help. Sometimes he simply doesn't know how.*

Your husband may not go with the furniture. He may act like a man in every sense of the word. His idiosyncrasies may drive you bonkers, like leaving toenail clippings on the bathroom floor. But if he's a good man—not self-centered, a drinker, a carouser, an abuser, a womanizer, etc.—he's your best bet to de-stress your life.

There are a few key things you need to know about him first, though.

He Wants to Be Your Hero

Your husband wants to be your hero. He wants to help. Sometimes he simply doesn't know how to help, and frankly, he's a little intimidated by you. You're the master juggler; he can usually just keep one ball in the air. So at times he thinks he's not really needed in your world. After all, it looks like you've got things pretty much under control, right?

But then one thing goes wrong, and all your well-laid plans for the day are blown sky-high. What do you do then? Run harder and faster? Or call your husband for some instant relief? He'll take time off work to get his son to trombone lessons when you've got the flu. He'll volunteer to go to the local marsh or wetland on a field trip on a rainy day with 56 fourth graders. And he'll even supply the snack for all of them like you had planned to. (What fourth grader knows the difference between store-bought and homemade cookies anyway?)

With just a little encouragement, you've got a wonderful resource that will make all the difference in your world—and your son will get to have a much more involved daddy too!

Just a Little Goes a Long Way

There are three things your man craves from you, and if you provide them for him, he'll knock down walls for you.

He Needs Your Respect

Have you ever asked a man a question and his answer is, "I don't know—ask the boss"? By that he means his wife. The sad thing is, sometimes he's joking, sometimes he's not.

But often that's exactly how men feel. Like their wives are in charge and capable enough, thank you, and the men aren't good enough around the house to really help out. So what happens when they get home? They get the "There there, boy, just go off and play" shuffle, as if they're puppies who are slightly naughty and need to be put in their outdoor doghouses before they make a mess on the floor.

How do you think your husband feels? Is he an integral part of your household, or merely an added appendage and something else to deal with when he gets home?

Your son is watching your relationship between you and your husband. He's using it to gauge how men act and how women act when they're married. Would you want your son to have the same type of marriage you have?

Ouch. That's where the rubber really meets the road, isn't it? Do you show your husband respect? Do you have an egalitarian relationship, where you are both equal partners in parenting, even though you play differing roles? Or are you calling all the shots in the home since you assume your husband isn't capable?

Your husband won't do things like you do. But he needs to know that you think he's competent.

Your husband won't do things like you do. But he needs to know that you think he's competent, just like your son does. He may not get the baby diapered quite the same way you do (and it may be slightly askew on the kid's bottom), but as long as it holds the goods, what does it matter in the long run? His dinner for the kids may consist of all "yellow" foods—macaroni and cheese, corn, and orange juice—instead of the colorful array you'd put on their plates, but it's still a nutritious dinner with all the food groups, isn't it?

He Needs to Be Needed

If you are too competent, your guy can think he's not really needed around the house. After all, if you can get it all done and do things faster than him, what is he good for anyway?

Your husband needs to be invited into your world. That may sound strange, but it's true. What you do during the day—all the things you manage simultaneously—are like a foreign world to him. The to-do list that you rattle off is like a foreign language to him, and he hasn't been given the translation book. He needs to be clued in as to what it all means and what you need from him. He wants you to ask for help. Then he can ride in on his manly steed and provide just that.

> *Men are wired to be problem solvers. That's one of the things they do best.*

Men are wired to be problem solvers. That's one of the things they do best. They like to focus on one problem and think through all the angles until they come to a solution. And you? You're thinking about at least 15 things at once, so you can only give each of them a cursory look before you have to move on to the next item on your to-do list.

Why not harness your male's need to be needed and his natural problem-solving ability to help not only in raising your son but also with other issues in the home?

He Needs to Be Fulfilled

Your husband needs to know that he's your number one man. That you put him first. This is important for your son to see too—that a child's needs don't supersede a husband's needs. It helps to give children the correct perspective of the pecking order in the house. That means when Dad comes home, Mom stops what she's doing and gives Dad a hug and a kiss and welcomes him home.

And what man wouldn't be an eager helper if he knew that helping would mean a less tired wife who was a more eager partner in bed?

I know what you're thinking. *Dr. Leman, is that all guys think about? Sex? Come on!*

As I often say, "No, they think about ESPN too."

Seriously, though, physical touch is the core of a man's needs. If he can't bond physically with you, his wife, he will feel a distance from you that will grow. He knows that you're busy with the kids and that they sap your energy. But if there's never any energy left to fulfill your husband, he will become a defeated man who, frankly, will make your life miserable. Just a little physical touch, though, and you've got a loyal man who's willing to do your bidding.

Let's say you come home from work exhausted. You know the kids trashed the house last night, and you haven't had time to pick up yet. You walk into the house and notice . . . a miracle. The kitchen's been cleaned up, trash and all. The counters are sparkling. And you even smell barbecue wafting from the backyard. All compliments of your happy husband—and your short little tryst from the night before. What would the smart woman do? She would walk up to her man, hug him from behind, kiss his neck, and say, "Oh, honey, thank you so much. I'm dog tired tonight. Thanks for all you're doing!"

Bet that man will come up with new ways to please you! And I bet your son will notice too, even if he thinks Mom and Dad are being "gross" and "gushy."

You see, marriage isn't about you. It's about the other person. It's about both of you together. In parenting, both of you have something to give, and that something is very different. But if your husband feels he is respected, needed, and fulfilled, he'll do anything for you. If you give a little, you'll be amazed at what you get back.

Different Perspectives Can Be a Good Thing

Parenting's a tough job, and you need what I call "couple power." Two brains are better than one in resolving any parenting issue. Your husband will also see things from a different lens than you will. He might be stricter on your son because he has higher expectations (especially if your son is a firstborn).

If you're too easy on your son, you might be able to learn a thing or two from the way your husband handles him—especially since your husband isn't as likely to fall for the same manipulation tricks that your son pulls on you. If your husband is too hard on your son, he might be able to learn a thing or two from watching how you handle your kid. Your son can only gain from that type of shared parenting approach.

Harness his logical, analytical, 1-2-3 power.

So no matter where you've stood before, work on establishing a foundation that will last a lifetime. Ask your husband what he thinks; harness his logical, analytical, 1-2-3 power; and let him help you solve your problems, whether they have to do with your children specifically or with juggling how much you have to do.

Take Karyn, for example, who was feeling overwhelmed. Now that all her kids were in school, she had returned to work part-time. Things went fine for a while, then tax season hit. She knew things would be crazy only for a couple weeks, but they would *really* be crazy. Her husband's job didn't have specific seasons, so she asked him to help her come up with solutions. After they brainstormed the problem, they both slept on it.

In the morning, Ron offered a solution. "You know, honey, those two weeks aren't hectic for me. What about if you take the kids to school in the morning and I leave work early to pick them up? Then I'll cook dinner, get the kids fed and help with the homework, and keep a plate warm for you in the oven."

When the time came, Ron even took his help a step further. He had a bathrobe hot from the dryer ready for Karyn, and he prepared a lavender-scented bath to help her relax so she could get a good night's sleep. All because Karyn had included him in the brainstorming. She'd treated him with respect and showed that she needed him. And when those two weeks were over, she fulfilled him as well—by giving him the romantic surprise of his life!

He's a Male

There's nothing like stating the obvious, but your husband IS a male. Just by watching your husband's actions, your son will figure out, *Oh, THAT is what a man does. That's how he acts.*

If your son sees a close, loving relationship between you and your husband, he's more likely to have the same type of relationship with his future wife. After all, he'll have seen the best of all role models!

Your knight will polish up his armor for you if you give him the least bit of encouragement. No, he's not perfect, but neither are you. Life's not perfect either. But why not love and enjoy the man you chose to marry? Why not help him be the best dad he can possibly be?

Loser!

But what if you haven't married a good man? What if you've married someone who lies, cheats, steals, and is a womanizer, an abuser, and a whole host of other things?

What This Mom Did Right

Actor Tom Cruise's mother was determined to survive in spite of her difficult circumstances. Her husband, an electrical engineer, was an abusive bully who lost his job so many times that the family had to move several times a year, including moving to three completely different states and even a different country. Then Mom Cruise decided she'd had enough of her husband and left him. She took her son, Tom, and his three sisters back to her hometown in Kentucky. There she worked three jobs just to make ends meet. Her do-whatever-it-takes-to-make-it attitude rubbed off on her children so that they all became hardworking. Tom often says that his mom is "the source of his belief that he could make any kind of life for himself that he chose."[1]

Now that's one gutsy mama.

That man will be no help in raising your son. All he'll do is set up tension in your life that you and your son don't need. My advice? Dump the chump. Yes, you read that right. Frankly, it's better to have no male role model at all in the home than to have a negative role model who is harmful for the family.

The sad reality is that many people marry the wrong person. You might have too. If you're a pleaser, you might be married to an abusive controller. But you can't change others; you can only change yourself.

If you had to do it over, some of you wouldn't marry the same man. You're a strong woman, but unfortunately strong women sometimes marry controlling men. As the old German saying goes, "We get too late smart." And by then you have little kids and a jerk for a husband who can't keep his job as an engineer, and every morning you wake up thinking, *I can't do this anymore.* But somehow you find the strength to make the right moves, to

You can't change others; you can only change yourself.

protect your little cubs in the den, to work three jobs when your husband blows your grocery and insurance money.

But, Mom, I want to be clear. Yes, you made the choice to marry that man, and you bear the consequences of it. However, you also have to draw the line if he is being verbally or physically abusive in any way, or if he's having affairs. No woman should have to put up with that. You shouldn't either. It's time to get both yourself and your children out of that relationship.

Going It Alone

If you're a single mom, you've got some additional parenting challenges. I don't have to tell you what they are since you're right in the middle of them. You might have an ex hanging around (who might be helpful or might not). Or you might not have a man at all in your life. But I want to say something clearly: don't take responsibility for what isn't your fault.

You didn't expect your husband to walk out on you for some other woman or to go off to "find himself."

You didn't expect the phone call that told you your husband had been killed in an accident.

You didn't expect to end up pregnant by your boyfriend, who then didn't want anything to do with you or your child.

And now you and your son have to live with the fallout from these heart-wrenching experiences.

You can't do it all, but you can do what you need to in order to raise your son into a healthy, well-balanced adult. Think of it this way: you are singled out to believe in your child, and that puts you high on the scale of importance! It's through your eyes, your behavior, your words, and your

---

The Single-Parent Thrive Plan

- Get back to the basics: take care of yourself and get some sleep.
- Be honest about what happened to get you where you are. How can things change if you don't know why they happened in the first place?
- Evaluate your priorities and write them down.
- Be ruthless about cutting your schedule to what's really doable.

---

thoughts that your son will learn about his self-worth, his strengths and weaknesses, and how to relate to others. What you do makes all the difference!

But I also want to be clear about something else. You're your son's *mom*. You're not his dad. Try to be both and you'll fail miserably, because your son is no dummy. But be his mom and work on keeping a heart connection with him, and you'll earn his respect and his love for the rest of his life.

Steady Goes It

How can you provide a stable environment for your son?

Only you know your son's heart and how he thinks. Only you know your particular situation. But here are some guidelines that will really help.

Tell the Truth—in Pieces

Your child doesn't need to know everything all at once about what happened to make him "lose Daddy" (the way many children think). When your child asks a question, make sure you first understand the question he's asking, not what you think he's asking. If you're not sure, ask him to clarify. Then tell the truth in love always, but tell it in pieces, age appropriately. The smartest thing to do is to answer the exact question your child has—no more, no less—at that moment. Then wait for the next question.

Let Your Child Talk and Remember

If your husband died, or if you divorced and your son remembers his daddy who used to be involved in his life, it's important to let him bring up memories and talk about the daddy who is now missing from his life. Don't ever dis your ex in front of your son. When your son gets old enough, he can figure out for himself what his father is really like—both good traits and bad traits. He doesn't need you harping on men. That can lead your son to think, *Okay, so men are bad. I'm a boy. I'm going to be a man. Am I bad?*

If your husband died, make sure your son has a picture of him and his daddy at eye level. Talk about the fun times you all had together and how much his daddy loved him. Talk about how you miss him too and how he'd love to be with the two of you right now.

Admit Your Mistakes

None of us is perfect. And if you got pregnant outside of marriage, your "mistake" stares you in the face every day. (However, let me clarify that your child is never a mistake. He is created in all his wonderful intricacies by a loving God to be exactly who he is.) You had met a guy who had about as much integrity and morals as a pea. Especially in your son's teen years, it's important for you to admit that you let your hopes, dreams, and hormones get the best of you, and it's made life more difficult. That's why you want something different for your child.

Don't let guilt control your decisions: *Well, I blew it, so who am I to tell my kid not to blow it?* Mom, you're *exactly* the person to talk to your son about sex before marriage, because you're living the results of that every day.

Realize You Will Butt Heads

You will butt heads with your son—especially if the two of you are the same birth order. It's only natural for two people (or more) living in a house to not always agree with each other. What's important is how you handle that disagreement. Set up an environment and guidelines for both of you to talk things out with mutual respect, rather than handling

> *Don't let guilt control your decisions.*

skirmishes with yelling, withdrawing, or threatening. And when you blow it with your son? Go to him first. (After all, *you* are the adult!) Your son needs to know that he is a human being worthy of respect. If you lose it, admit that, apologize, and ask your son to forgive you. Then let him do the same at his tough moments.

Hold Your Ground

Many single moms struggle with being too permissive, because they feel guilty there's no daddy for their son. So they let their sons get away with unacceptable behavior. (Translate: their sons become brats!) You can't turn back the clock. You can't undo what's happened already in your son's life. But you can go forward. Remember this statement from earlier in the book? "Love and discipline—you can't have one without the other." It's absolutely true. Within boundaries, there is safety. Outside of boundaries, anything can happen. Do your best to walk the authoritative path.

Take Breaks . . . for You

In homes with two-parent families, you as a mom can take breaks—even if they're as short as a bubble bath all by yourself for an hour. If you're a single parent, those breaks can be much harder to find. But, Mom, you've got to take some. No parent can be "on" 24-7. It's too exhausting physically and emotionally. In order to be your best for your son, you need to take small breaks.

Make Your Son Your Priority

Your son will be the age he is for only so long. Right now you are your son's psychological balance. You're the one he needs to make his world right. He doesn't need stuff like all the other kids have (so don't guilt yourself into working lots of extra hours to see he gets it or to "replace" his father). He needs your time and your energies. He needs to know that even though the world can be tough, Mom is always there.

> It's not your job to find a daddy for your son.

So get creative in your work options. Use Grandma and Grandpa or a beloved neighbor for child care, swap child care with a friend, or work part-time in an office and part-time from home. The sky's the limit in figuring out ways to spend as much time as possible with your son.

Focus on your connection with him and you'll never go wrong. It's not your job to find a daddy for your son. But it is your job to establish a home where your child feels safe.

But Doesn't My Son Need a Man in His Life?

There's a hole in your son's life. You feel it. Your child feels it.

You can't replace a dad in your son's life, but it's important for your son to have healthy role models. Consistent role models.

In-N-Out burgers are incredibly wonderful. I'd drive anywhere to find one. But in-and-out daddies? They're devastating to a child. If your ex is around and can be that *consistent* role model for your son, terrific. (It can and does happen for some couples who divorce. But the majority of couples who divorce have experienced so much tension between them that this isn't likely.)

Your son needs someone to do boy/man things with him, like fishing, playing baseball, and talking about girls. If you have a brother or a father who can provide that for him and they already have a relationship, fabulous! Just extend that relationship a little further by providing opportunities for your son to have more time with that person. Or what about a man from church who has little boys of his own? Why not ask him if he'd be willing to include your son on an outing, such as a camping trip?

Communities often have Big Brother programs as well. One single guy I know has been a Big Brother to the same boy, Alfonso, for the past three years. Alfonso's own father has emotional problems and isn't able to be there in his son's life, so Alfonso waits with great anticipation each week for Sunday to roll around, when he and "Uncle Dave" always spend the afternoon together.

Some opportunities will come up naturally. Others you have to hunt for. But here's the good news in the interim: if I could choose the ideal parent-child combination for single parents, it would be a mother with a boy or a father with a girl. Why do I say that? Once again, it's because the opposite-sex relationships are the ones that have the most significant impact in a family.

Most of us have been duped into thinking that the most special relationship is between same-sex parents and children. That's why we have all those mother-daughter banquets and father-son camping trips. But the relationships that carry the most psychological punch and form the child the most are the mother-son and father-daughter relationships.

Through your actions and words, you're communicating to your son what you see and admire most in men. And guess who's listening and watching? That's why you, Mom, are so important. Even if it does mean you have to pick those creepy-crawly critters out of your son's pockets.

Some opportunities will come up naturally. Others you have to hunt for.

Daddies are important too. They make indelible imprints on their sons. When you have an active, involved daddy who balances discipline and love, your son has a role model for a lifetime. When you don't, you have to work a little harder to provide opportunities for healthy male influences. Your son needs a man in his life to show him the ropes on how to be a man, to help him become comfortable in his male body.

But whether your son has a daddy in his life or not, you can build his self-worth, show him that actions have consequences, establish in him a strong work ethic, and help him gain a tender heart.

Someday your son will grow up and become a man. What kind of man do you want him to be? What values do you want him to carry with him to his dying day?

What You Can Do

- Realize you can't do it all, and you can't do it all alone.
- Gather support from men for your parenting journey.
- Remember that no one can run 24-7. So take a break. You'll be happier, and so will your son. In fact, he'll thank you for doing it.

As for this man, when I die, I don't need a Super Bowl ring, a 50-year watch from a company, or a huge portfolio to tell me that I have worth and I've done a good job. All I want is a family who looks at me and says, "I love you and I miss you. We sure had some great times together, didn't we?"

11

Are You "Velcro Woman"?

You're mighty, but you're only one woman. So how can you juggle everything? Here are hints for sorting out what's important from what's not.

I t's a typical morning in your house.

5:30 a.m. You drag yourself out of bed to start the coffee perking, then race to the computer to finish online research for your new project at work and to order your son's birthday present. (His birthday is in two days.)

6:30 a.m. You drink your third cup of coffee in between packing three of your children's lunches—snacks as well for the younger two—and begin to feel the caffeine jitters. But that's okay, because it only makes you work faster. You even remember to pack your third-grade son's soccer outfit, the money you need to donate for his teacher's gift, and the new pencils he forgot to take yesterday. And for your

213

kindergartener? Oh, yeah, you better pack an extra set of clothes since she fell in the mud yesterday, so it's better safe than sorry.

7:00 a.m. You have waffles in the toaster and orange juice poured by the time your seventh-grade son stumbles his way down the stairs. He grabs the half-cooked waffle and slugs down the juice before grabbing his backpack and racing out the door. "Hey, you forgot your—" you begin to yell, then run out the door to fling the item at him so he can catch the bus on time.

7:10 a.m. Your husband stumbles down the stairs, bleary-eyed, and asks where his shirt for work is. You race to the dryer and grab the shirt you washed just last night. You give it a quick pass with the iron, then hand it to your husband as he's grabbing his waffle and coffee and heading out the door.

> *"Hey, you forgot your—"*

7:15 a.m. Your mother calls to ask you when your son's concert is and to share her concern about your dad. You don't want to hurt her feelings and cut her off, so you try to listen even though your brain is racing with your to-do list and you're on borrowed time before your one-year-old wakes up. Your third grader is eating waffles and asking if you've packed his soccer outfit.

7:30 a.m. Your mother-in-law calls to tell you what you did wrong at the last family dinner and how you're not treating her son right.

7:31 a.m. The baby wakes up and starts to cry. You change her diaper—and it's a big, bad one—and soothe her while still listening to your mother-in-law's harping.

7:41 a.m. Your mother-in-law finally runs out of words and hangs up. But before she does, she tells you, "You know, honey, I'm only telling you this because I love you, and I love my son." *Yeah, right*, you think.

7:50 a.m. You're feeding the baby Cheerios to keep her happy while you mix her cereal, when suddenly you realize what time it is. You race upstairs to wake up your kindergartener, who must have fallen asleep after her third-grade brother woke her up. The baby, who's sitting on your hip, trails Cheerios all the way down the hallway and up the stairs.

8:00 a.m. Your kindergartener eats waffles, pooh-poohs the orange juice, and insists on chocolate milk. You make it but say she can drink it in the car on the way to school, because there isn't time.

8:10 a.m. You've managed to get the third grader, the kindergartener, the baby, all the snacks, the lunches, and various paraphernalia in the car, after having the kindergartener wander off twice to find a toy.

8:25 a.m. You drop your third grader off, wave good-bye, then head for the kindergarten door to drop your daughter off. She can't get her coat zipped, so you climb over the front seat of the minivan to help her, since the baby screams if you get out of the car without her.

8:28 a.m. You wave your kindergartener good-bye and look at your watch. Just enough time to get to the doctor's office for your baby's one-year checkup at 9:00.

Mom, in just a few hours you've already accomplished what 10 men wouldn't even attempt to do in a week. And that doesn't even begin to make a dent in your day!

All Stressed Out and Nowhere to Go

Everybody has stress. There's the kind of stress you get when you slam on the brakes in traffic and almost hit a car. Adrenaline rushes through your body and you feel like your heart is in your throat. But within 20 minutes, your heart rate is back to normal.

Then there's a different kind of stress—the kind that just never goes away, and it often grows bigger and bigger. It's the stress of being Velcro Woman—the woman everything and everyone sticks to. No matter how hard you try to shake it, it never goes away. It's the kids, the lack of time, the annoying husband that can put you over the edge. It's like going to the mall to shop all day and leaving the lights on in your car. When you come out nine hours later, the car won't start. The battery is exhausted.

One of the most difficult things about being a woman in America today is that everyone wants a piece of you.

Ever read the newspaper, magazine, or online news accounts about entertainers collapsing on stage? They're hospitalized for exhaustion.

Moms are, in my opinion, the wonders of the universe. They can leap tall buildings in a single bound, they can go where no person has gone before, and they can somehow get toddlers to eat. The problem is that mothers are also some of the most stressed people on the planet. There's just so much to do and not enough of them. No doubt you are mighty . . . but there's only one of you.

Have you started to feel like Velcro Woman? Are you feeling drained emotionally and physically, trying to meet everyone's needs at once? It's no wonder! You're trying to be mom, cook, chauffeur, wife (if you're married), bottle washer, laundry doer . . . in short, miracle worker. But it all adds up to an awful lot to do.

One of the most difficult things about being a woman in America today is that everyone wants a piece of you. Your boss wants that memo. The kids want you to get to three different locations, stat, and in order to do so, you'd have to become a time traveler, because their events all happen in the next hour. Your church only wants "one evening" of yours a week; they say that's all they'll need to help launch the new ministry they're hoping you'll be a part of. (But secretly you have the feeling it's going to take a lot more than that.) And, of course, to help save up for your son's college, you're running a typing and proofing business on the side.

Just listing a woman's multitasking abilities makes me tired. I think *I* need to sit down and rest.

Since women focus more on relationships, they will always find themselves juggling more than men. Do we men care if somebody doesn't like us? If someone's feelings will be hurt if we turn them down? If one of our kids thinks it's not fair because we can't do everything on his agenda?

Nope. We men just shrug and say, "Hey, that's life. Sometimes people aren't going to like you." But can you say that? Not as easily, because you care what people think of you. Your pleasing mentality kicks in, so you try even harder to get it all done.

But after a while, you're like that gerbil in a cage, running and running and running on that wheel and feeling like you're never getting anywhere. Even worse, the next day you wake up and do it all over again!

The "You Can Do It All" Trap

Nobody can do it all. You can try, but you'll fail. It's just not humanly possible. We all have the same 24 hours in a day, but somehow moms are able to squeeze about 48 hours out of each day. It's a miracle I've never quite figured out.

217

But the majority of moms will pay the price in exhaustion. The sooner you realize and tell yourself you can't do it all, the better off you'll be. Then you can make a conscious effort to change things.

Maybe you won't be the Martha Stewart of your neighborhood anymore. But why do you think you should be anyway? Most folks don't know the difference between Betty Crocker brownies and ones you spent an hour making from scratch. Kids eat them just as fast.

Your figure may droop a bit more in the middle because you're no longer getting to the gym a couple times a week with your girlfriends, but in the end we all droop, don't we? How about a fast walk around the block with your dog and your son to take the edge off the stress of his school day? He'll have a chance to detox, he'll see you care about his day, and you'll get some fresh air for a breather.

The sooner you realize and tell yourself you can't do it all, the better off you'll be.

So why not lower your own high-jump bar of life? After all, who do you think put it there?

It all starts with one little word.

What Would It Take to Get You Off That Gerbil Wheel?

There's a powerful word you should try using: *no*.

If you don't want to be in a certain situation, simply say no. You're going to be bombarded all day, every day, with things as seemingly innocuous as being asked to be the chairwoman of the women's bazaar at church or the neighborhood block party or garage sale.

Let's say someone calls you on the phone and asks you to help out. For nine consecutive years you've said yes. But each year, for weeks prior to the event, your family hears you lamenting about how much work it is and how you don't want to do it. Here's my advice: just say no.

Give no explanation, since if you begin to explain, then Mary Jane, the person calling, will find a way to rebut why you can't do it and will talk you into it. If you say, "Well, my husband's work has changed, so I'm needing to work more and I wouldn't have the time to head it up," that gives Mary Jane the opportunity to say, "Well, wait a minute. What if I got Judy Jones to help you? She just moved here and is so creative and artistic. She could help you with so many of the projects. It would lighten your load tremendously." But then you end up being the cochair of the event and working with a woman who is new at it, so it takes even more time. And what have you accomplished? Nothing.

There's a powerful word you should try using: no.

Instead, just say a simple, "Thanks for calling, Mary Jane, but I'm not in a position to be able to help this year."

Be firm and get yourself off the phone quickly.

No is a powerful word, and it can change your stress level almost instantaneously.

Try it. You'll have a tough time forming the word for a while, but when you get used to it, you'll like it. I promise.

Whose Agenda Are You Living By?

Are you doing what you want to be doing, or doing it just because it's expected of you? And who is expecting it of you anyway? Is it another person? Or are those expectations all your own?

Well, my mom worked when we kids were little, so I should be able to handle it too.

Just because your mom did it, does that mean you have to? Are you wired exactly the same way as your mom? Do you have the same energy level?

My neighbor has the perfect kids. They're always so polite and well mannered. I wish I could train my kids to be like that.

But were you there in the hallway with your neighbor last night when her son screamed, "I hate you!" and slammed his door?

Life isn't always greener on the other side of the fence. And you'd have to mow the grass just like you do on your side.

My sister spends a lot of time with her kids. She has them in all the best programs. They're always involved in a concert, a ball game, a racquetball tournament, or a spelling bee.

Okay, so on the outside your sister looks successful and her kids look happy and busy. But are you there late at night when she takes a sleeping pill because it's the only way she can rest without thinking of what's next on her to-do list? Do you really want to get your son into the rat race of life more quickly by signing him up for every available program so he won't "miss out"? But what is he really missing out on? More stress? And what are you missing out on? Drive-through dinners because you're never at home? A car whose gas tank is empty?

Beware of the activity trap. Your son is not going to be more successful in life just because you have him in swim class, Boy Scouts, soccer, and karate all in one year. All you're doing is raising a son who thinks he has to go from activity to activity to please you and to be someone of worth. It sets him up later in life to think he has to do more, *be* more, to actually be someone. And he won't be able to relax and enjoy life, even on vacation.

What This Mom Did Right

When I found out I was pregnant, I really wrestled with what to do about working. I loved my job, and I didn't want to give it up. But I also loved this child growing inside me.

When my son was born, I was overjoyed. I had 12 weeks of maternity leave, then had to go back to work. I spent the first 6 weeks crying every time I had to leave him in day care. I had no idea how hard it would be for me to leave my son.

One day it hit me: I could do something to change this. So I talked with my husband and my employer, and we worked out a plan. My husband got the approval to work from home one day a week, and I spent that day in the office. My husband loved spending time with Ethan, and I knew our little boy was being well cared for. My office got me a laptop so I could work four afternoons from home, and the other four mornings Ethan got to spend with his grandma while I worked.

Dr. Leman, you were right. Creative options really do work, and they also took us through a rough financial time when my husband was making the transition from working in the office to starting his new at-home business.

Desiree, California

Stress is a natural part of life. It'll never completely go away. And some stress is good because it's motivating. It helps us get things done. But why on earth would you go out of your way to heap more of it on yourself? Why are you competing with someone else anyway? Let the "someone elses" do what they want to, but you do what you need to because it's best for your family.

Priorities Is Not a Dirty Word

Right now I want you to make a list of the activities that are on your to-do list for tomorrow.

Go ahead. Write them down. I'll wait. . . .

Prioritize!

- Make a list of everything that's on your schedule for this week.
- Divide that list into three columns:
  - Must Do
  - Don't Have to Do But Would Like to Do
  - Things I Hate Doing, and Maybe Someone Else Could Do
- Take the "Must Do" column and cut it in half, keeping the most important priorities.
- Do those remaining "Must Do" items for a week, ignore the others (or arrange for someone else to do them), and see what happens to your stress level.

Okay, got them?

Now get another piece of paper and write down the top three things from your list that you *must* get done tomorrow.

Let's take a good look at your lists.

If one item you wrote down is "grocery shop," since it's been three weeks since you went, I agree with you. Groceries are a priority. Everybody in the family gets cranky when they're hungry.

If one thing is "clean the sunporch," ask yourself, *Is that really necessary? Sure, I'm having a party on Saturday, but would it kill anyone if I have one room that's messy?*

If another thing is "pick up Randy after his play practice," ask yourself, *Do I always need to be the one who picks him up? Another guy in the play lives only a couple blocks away. Hmm, maybe I'll call his mom and see if we can switch off nights picking up the boys. That would save me 40 minutes a night.*

Ah, now your priority list is working for you. The idea is to get creative and see what you really have to do, what you don't have to do, and what you can ask for help on.

Got Guilt?

If you're evaluating everything that you do during the day and starting to sort out your highest priorities and what you can let go, something's going to happen.

You're going to be flooded with guilt.

But I can't not go to that lunch, you think. *I'll really offend my friends!*

If you have friends like that, then I'm sorry for you. Get some new ones.

But Justin really wants to play soccer this year. And he's so good at baseball.

Fine, then let the boy pick one activity and call it a day.

But Wednesday is always the night I run him to his friend's house to study.

What? His friend's parent can't drive every other week? And why does your kid have to go to a friend's house to study anyway? Couldn't he just study at home?

See what I mean? See how easy it is to allow yourself to be manipulated by guilt? And don't believe for a minute that you're the only one who knows that. Your son is a master manipulator—yes, as cute as he is. And he's got your number.

"Mom, I *have* to go to that party. Everybody's going! All I have to bring is some soda."

But just because *everybody* is going (that word alone ought to be your flag that it's not the truth), does that mean your son has to be there too? Especially if you're not sure if the parents will be at the party, and you don't know them very well anyway? And if it means you need to run to the store to pick up soda that he *has* to have for the party?

Friends can do a masterful job of pushing those buttons too. So can husbands, exes, and boyfriends. The question is, are you going to allow yourself to be manipulated by guilt into trying to do everything, or are you going to sit down and carefully decide what is realistically doable?

One way, you stay on the gerbil wheel. The other way, you get off and you stay off. Then you can finally look at life without that dizzy feeling you get from being constantly on the go.

The Work-or-Not Quandary

Should you work outside the home or not? And if so, full-time or part-time? (If you're a single parent, you probably don't have a choice because you're the sole breadwinner. But you can still consider these issues in regard to the type of job you go after and the location from which you work.) You as a family need to make that decision for yourselves, taking into account your personalities, energy levels, and income levels. But just remember, Mom, that working outside the home will take its greatest toll on *you*. That's because what you expect of yourself won't change instantly—you'll have to reprioritize everything you did before you started working—and you'll still feel that tug to "be all" for your spouse and children, not to mention your parents, grandparents, place of worship, etc.

One way, you stay on the gerbil wheel. The other way, you get off and you stay off.

If you're considering starting a home business or working full-time or part-time outside the home, here are some good questions to ask.

What's Your Energy Level?

Some people naturally have more energy than others. They don't need as much sleep, they can handle a lot more activities, they're superb multitaskers, and they find great joy in interacting with others outside the home. If that's you, you may be a good candidate for working some hours outside the home. But if the idea of working full-time or part-time exhausts you just thinking about it, and you have a hard time juggling other life tasks in your day (laundry, meals, etc.) while taking care of your children's needs, you may need to decide that now is not the time to make that transition.

What Are the Ages, Stages, Needs, and Personalities of Your Children?

It's fairly easy to get a few hours of work in at home when children are young and take two naps a day. But what about when they get sick and you're up with them all night, and you can't even think about getting your project done? When children go down to one nap, working from home gets tougher. And after they drop that nap and before they go to school, the times to work from home are few and far between. But when your child gets to kindergarten, if he's there from 9 to 12, you may be able to work for a couple hours a day during that time. If he's in full-day kindergarten or he's an older child, you have the entire school day (about six hours by the time you shuttle the child back and forth to school or get him on and off the bus). Just keep in mind that when your work at your workplace is over, you still have the responsibility of meeting your child's needs at home and the domestic responsibilities of running a household.

Also, some children are quiet book readers; others are constant movers. Some are independent; others are clingy.

Only you can judge the age, stage, needs, and personality of your son. The most important thing is that you allow

225

yourself to be flexible from year to year. What works now may not work in a year.

How Much Would Day Care Cost?

Working can be financially beneficial to your family, but it's not necessarily so, depending on how much you're getting paid, how much gas it takes to travel to your job, and how much the child care costs (part-time, full-time, in-home, at a day-care center). So check out the costs carefully.

Here's what one mom discovered: "In the Chicago area, it costs me $8 an hour for child care at my friend's house. That means it costs $64 for me to spend a full day in the office. If I make $15 an hour, that basically means I'm working for $7 an hour, minus the gas and time it takes to get my child back and forth to my friend's. I've had to ask myself, *Is that worth it? To be away from my child for a whole day while making only about $5 an hour, by the time I count transportation costs and lunch?*"

The possibilities are endless. But only you can choose what's best for your child.

If you need to consider day care, make sure you think of all options. Perhaps you could stay home full-time with your child but use naptimes for some work, or use a neighbor girl after school to entertain your child for an hour. You could use day care part-time or full-time, get some help from Grandma and Grandpa for part-time babysitting, job share, or use a church-run day care that you're more comfortable with and a place where your child is used to going. Or perhaps your husband can work from home some days while you freelance. Maybe your husband even has the temperament to handle colic, runny noses, and changing diapers all day and still wear a smile. If so, and if he can put a hold on his career to stay home so you can continue your job (and the two of you agree on that), then bless the man! The more full-time care a child can have from at least one parent, the better.

In other words, the possibilities are endless. But only you can choose what's best for your child. After all, you're the one who signed on for your son's all-day care when he came into your life. Nobody can raise your son like you.

What Else Would You Be Giving Up or Changing?

When women go back to work with children in the house, other things change as well. Home-cooked dinners often become microwave dinners, fast food, or quick fixes simply because there are only so many hours in a woman's day. There's nothing wrong with a microwave dinner (other than more fat and sodium, unless you're a watchful shopper), but cooking from scratch is usually a lot cheaper. Bills for clothing go up, since you now have to maintain a professional wardrobe instead of the T-shirts and jeans that have baby spittle on them. And ten casual outfits can cost the same as one professional outfit. You'll also find yourself filling the car with gas more often. When all is said and done, these hidden costs can add up to an awful lot more than you think.

Why Do You Really Want to Work?

Do you work because your family needs the extra money to pay for necessities (such as groceries, bills, health insurance) or your husband lost his job? Is it because you're considering going back to your career and trying to break back into the working world? Is it because you need time away from home

227

What You Can Do

- Take a walk and think through what's most important to you.
- Consider your personality and energy level.
- Be ruthless with your Day-Timer or Blackberry. (It won't get offended.)
- List your top three priorities and keep a copy of them where you can see them every day.

---

and an outlet for your creative energies? Is it because without working, you don't feel like you're contributing enough to the family, or you are seen just as the "wifey" and "stay-at-home mommy" who's low on the totem pole?

Being aware of your motivations to work can help you make a solid, informed decision—and one that will be healthy for your child as well.

Being a mom is a full-time job in itself. A real job. Even if you don't get a paycheck and you never get a vacation.

But the rewards are long lasting.

What If . . .

Let's say you go for your standard yearly checkup at the doctor and you get a phone call to go back to see him. "I hate to tell you this," the doctor says when you're seated in his office, "but you have Stage 2 ovarian cancer."

What thoughts would first go through your mind at such news?

I can guarantee it wouldn't be, *Oh no, what is the New Year's gala committee going to do without me?* or, *I guess I won't be finishing my project at work now, will I?*

Chances are good your first thoughts will be of your family. *What if I die? What will they do without me?*

All the activities in the world won't matter at such a time. What will matter? Your relationships with the people you love most. The people who are the most important to you.

When it comes down to the wire, your relationship with your son is what matters. If you major on that and minor on everything else, you'll have a relationship with your son that can weather any storms.

—— 12 ——

Your Someday Man

Someday the little boy with the bandaged knees
and that mouthy, hormone-laden teenager will
become a man. But the work you do now to cap-
ture his heart will pay off—just wait and see.

When I was a little boy, my mother always made me
tomato soup with a dab of butter on top. To this day,
I can still see that butter spreading out over the top of my
soup. Mmm-mmm, good! And she always served that deli-
cious tomato soup with warm grilled-cheese sandwiches. I
loved the way that meal tasted.

One day Mom had a lot on her plate to do, so she asked me,
"Do you think you could make your own soup and sandwich?"

My face fell. "Well, I suppose I could, but it sure tastes
better when you make it, Mom."

I wasn't just buttering her up (no pun intended). In my
little boy mind, that meal really did taste better because my
mother made it *just for me*.

That's all she needed to hear. She set aside what she was doing and made me a lunch I'll never forget.

You see, it's our perception of things that makes a difference. Did that soup and sandwich *really* taste better just because Mom made it? No, it was your standard tomato soup and typical grilled cheese. But because in my mind they tasted better, that became my reality.

If you grew up in a healthy home, you know you were loved and you realize that your parent(s) made a lot of sacrifices on your behalf. Some sacrifices were little—putting down the paper to teach you how to throw a baseball, or being asked to "help" your mom bake some cookies, even though she knew it would take twice as long doing it *with* you as doing it *for* you. Other sacrifices were bigger, such as your mom moonlighting with freelance work for a couple hours each night after you went to bed, or not buying herself clothes so she could buy you new shoes. Or driving her beater van for yet another year so you would have some money for college.

> *You see, it's our perception of things that makes a difference.*

But all too many of you grew up in homes where you felt like you didn't matter. Where your parents treated you like you were just "something else to take care of" because they were either struggling with the traumas of their own growing-up years or too busy focusing on their career to give you the time of day.

Harvard sociologist Robert Putnam estimates that "families have meals together about one-third less often today than they did in the mid 1970s." He also believes that "parents are about one-third less likely to take vacations, watch television, or even chat with their children."[1]

What This Mom Did Right

Elvis Presley always said that the most important woman in his life was his mother, according to ElvisPresleyNews.com. Gladys Love Presley was also the most influential person in his life since she encouraged his talent from when he was very young. Though Gladys's life was far from easy—her husband went to jail for three years for forging a check when Elvis was three—she continued to encourage her son in his career, even though she worried about his fame. With his first royalty check for his music, Elvis bought his mother a pink Cadillac.[2]

Is this something that's happening in your home? If so, why not reverse the trend? *Nobody can raise your child like you can.* And what your son wants most is to connect with you. He longs for your approval.

As you make your way along the journey as mother and son, here are a few things to remember.

Bye-Bye, Perfect

Never forget that training your son takes time, and the standard isn't perfection. When you cook a meal, is it always perfect? When you parallel park your car, is it the regulation eighteen inches away from the sidewalk, both tires equally distant from the curb? When you iron a pair of pants, is every pleat perfectly creased?

I doubt it. You're not perfect, and neither is your child. And there's no such thing as a perfect day. Kids will get grumpy; you'll get crabby. You'll both say things that you don't mean because a relationship is fluid. You have to figure things out along the way. You might have two sons, and your relationship with them could be as different as night and day. But if you focus on the *relationship* and connecting with your son, you won't go wrong.

When you make a mistake, apologize, then go on. When he makes a mistake, extend the same grace to him as you'd like for yourself.

Don't expect him to do things perfectly. Keep a check on your critical eye. After all, could you walk in a straight line the first time you tried to walk? Or did you waver all over the place until your legs got strong enough to hold you up? Your son is trying out his legs now too, no matter what age he is. He needs to be confident that Mom is behind him to pick him up as needed and to encourage him to go on. Note that he doesn't need you to hover, to constantly tell him what he's doing wrong. Nor does he need you to say, "Well, you could have done that better." Instead, he needs your nurturing, loving, unconditional presence to make his world safe and allow him to be able to take risks that will help him mature and grow.

Most kids are pushed too hard today by moms and dads who want them to excel at everything they do. But that's unrealistic. There's always someone else who can top what your kid can do. You'll never win by playing the competition game, like this one:

First mom: "My child walked at 14 months."

Second mom: "My child walked at 11 months."

First mom: "Well, Andrew said his first word at nine months."

Second mom: "Scotty was potty trained at that age."

Don't get into the game of one-upmanship. Parenting your son isn't a race to see who can get to the end faster. It's about the slow, steady journey along the way and the connection of hearts.

So why not accept your child as he is, with his particular set of strengths and weaknesses? Why not let him risk and experience failure within the safety of your nest? After all, it's how we handle losing—more than how we handle winning—that defines our character.

Just Say No

We talked about this before, but I want to reemphasize it because it's so important. Don't fall into the trap of thinking that you have to run your son from activity to activity so that he can compete with what everyone else is doing and rise to the top of his class, or else he won't get into the right college or be successful in life. Your son also doesn't need as much stuff as you think he does.

I don't want to pick on Mickey Mouse too much, but when you take your son to Disneyland at age two, buy him Mickey ears, a Woody T-shirt, an Aladdin sword, Lion King pajamas, and Donald Duck sunglasses, and you push your stroller the length of California, don't be surprised if he's *not* a happy camper by the end of the day. And most likely, you won't be a happy camper either, because you've just spent your wad of vacation money for the next couple years, and you're going to have to work overtime to pay the Visa bills.

Kids don't need activities. They don't need stuff. They need you, Mom. Your time. Your love. Your perspective. Your listening ear. Your comfort. Your wisdom.

Build Up His Self-Worth

Instead of worrying about building up your son's self-esteem, work on his self-worth. Don't say, "Oh, what a great kid you

What's Good about Mom

When I polled men from ages 20 to 60 about their moms, here's what they had to say:

"She never gave up on me."

"She taught me what was most important about life."

"She never thought I was stupid . . . even when I was."

"She believed the best of me, always."

"She didn't put up with baloney, even though I handed her a lot of it!" (said while laughing)

"She never ragged on Dad, even when he left her. She's an amazing woman."

"She's the smartest woman I know."

"She taught me the practical basics of life."

"She was always consistent. What she said she'd do, she did."

"She was there at every one of my games, cheering whether I won or lost."

"She admitted when she was wrong."

"She always knew what to say . . . and when not to say anything."

are" (a focus on just the child). Instead, say, "I'm so proud of you for working so hard to learn that clarinet piece. I know playing the clarinet isn't easy for you, but you've stuck with it for six months. And wow, what a difference. Your work is really paying off." That will make your son work even harder on learning the clarinet, or anything else he attempts to do. But if you tell him he's wonderful even when he's not, he'll know you're lying and he won't trust other things you say either.

True encouragement means recognizing what your son does and acknowledging his actual accomplishments—whether those accomplishments take place in school, at home, or anywhere else. It's about noticing those things that deserve to be noticed and taking the time to mention them.

So point out when your son is doing something right. Notice his choices and actions. But shelve all that empty rah-rah, "you're such a great kid" kind of stuff.

Words Are a Powerful Thing

You hold a very powerful tool in your hand, Mom. Your words.

They can cause hurt that can be remembered for a lifetime:

"You're so dumb!"

"What is wrong with you? I thought you were smarter than that."

"You're just like your father! A loser!"

"Why I ever decided to have kids, I'll never know."

Or they can bring healing, comfort, or encouragement:

"Of all the sons in the world I could have, I'd choose you all over again if I could."

"When you stood up for that kid, I thought, 'I'm so proud of you, son.' I can't wait to tell Grandpa about what happened."

"There are so many things you could have chosen to do on a Saturday, but it means a lot to me that you decided to stay and help paint the porch. We got it done together so much faster, didn't we?"

There's no greater power in the world than words. They've started wars. They've stopped wars. They've built relationships. They've torn apart relationships. They've repaired relationships. When you open your mouth, you hold your son's welfare in your hands.

How are you using your words? Your little boy or big boy is so much more tender inside than you'll ever know. And the one he wants to please the most is you. What you say to him matters deeply and will be ingrained on the man he will become.

Focus on the ABCs

Remember the two groups of ABCs we talked about?

What is your child's *attitude* about life in general? About school? His friends? His family? You? Your child's attitude reveals his heart—what he really thinks about things. Does he have a giving heart or a gimme heart? How is that attitude reflected in his day-to-day *behavior*? And most of all, what is your son's *character*? Who is your son when no one is looking?

You're the parent, so be the parent.

Make sure your home is a place of *acceptance* and *belonging* and that your child knows you see him as *competent*. In the tumultuous adolescent years, that kind of home environment will do wonders to remove any rocks that crop up in your relationship. Your son needs to know that he is part of your family and that his opinion matters a great deal.

Walk the Authoritative Path

You're the parent, so be the parent. It's your job to walk that fine line of authoritative parenting, which focuses on love, consistency, and teaching, while allowing the child to experience the consequences of his actions.

Wishy-washy permissiveness allows your son to run over you and control the household. He won't like you any more than you'll like him in the long run. Things may seem to run smoothly for a while because he's getting what he wants, but look out down the road. Simply stated, if you can't stand up

> ### Ways to Win Your Boy's Heart
>
> - Let him be a boy—noisy, competitive, risk-taking.
> - Share his excitement when he learns something new.
> - Treat his heart with tender, loving care. (Remember, he's a softie underneath.)
> - Let him conquer whatever it is he wants to conquer.

for yourself, how can you expect your son to respect you? To respect *any* woman?

Don't set up your son—or any woman he dates or marries—for a fall. Your son needs to know that he's not the center of the universe. The earlier he finds that out, the better. Kids are born self-centered. They have to learn to care about others and how to share with and give to those who are needier. What better role model could they have than a mom who does that naturally?

And don't be the authoritarian parent who controls her child out of fear, shame, and embarrassment. Making your child obey won't capture his heart; it'll earn his resentment. And it will short-circuit any potential relationship you may have with your son down the line.

Love Does Make the World Go Round

Karina had just turned 31 when she was diagnosed with breast cancer. After a series of radiation and chemo treatments over a six-month period, she received the news: the treatments weren't working. So she and her husband agreed that she would have surgery to remove both breasts as well as the lymph nodes on both arms. It would be a delicate surgery and a painful recovery.

Karina's three young children missed their mommy. She'd been sick for the Christmas holidays, New Year's Day, Valentine's Day, and two of the children's birthdays, and now she'd be in the hospital again.

A week after her surgery, she was still in intense pain and on IVs. All of a sudden, by her bed she saw three chubby little fists, all holding rather crushed, wilted-looking red tulips.

"Mommy, Mommy!" one of her three-year-old twins said. "I wuv you!"

"Yeah, wuv you," said the less verbal twin.

Then the five-year-old chimed in. "Mommy, I missed you! Daddy let us pick flowers all by ourselves at the grocery store. Just 'cause we love you."

"Happy Mother's Day!" all three shouted at the top of their lungs.

It was the best Mother's Day Karina had ever had. She was alive and she was loved.

You see, everyone just wants to be loved. There's nothing better than that.

You'll make lots of sacrifices—your time, your money, your emotional and physical energy—as you invest in raising your son. But every moment you spend, every prayer you pray, every tear you shed, every laugh you share will pay in huge dividends. Maybe not right away, but someday. Because someday your boy will leave your nest and start collecting twigs and branches and leaves to make his own nest. And as he does, he'll remember the strategies on nest building that you taught him. He may not remember everything you did—and everything you didn't do—but he will certainly remember your love. And that same love will get passed to the little fledglings and the mommy fledgling in his own nest.

I guess love does indeed make the world go round.

Write It Down

Life is busy, but don't forget about what's really important.

- Write a note, a letter, or an email to your son, telling him, "I love you and I'm proud of you. Here's what I hope and pray for you." Then include your dreams and prayers for your son. Why not do it each year on his birthday as part of his birthday present?
- Keep a journal of your son's first words, funny phrases, and other things he does that are uniquely him.
- Slip your son a commercial: "I'm so proud to be your mom, and yesterday, when I found out you did X, Y, and Z, I thought that was so kind and sweet of you. You went the extra mile to help that person in trouble."

Your son will be smiling all over the place . . . whether he admits it to you or not.

It's All in the Perspective

Remember my story about my mom and the wonderful tomato soup and grilled-cheese sandwiches she used to make? Think about that story for a minute. As a guy in his sixties, I've eaten more than a few lunches in my lifetime. How many of those can I remember? Not very many. So why do I remember that one lunch in particular, eating that tomato soup with the melted butter on top? Because it has very warm feelings connected with my mom.

Someday your son is going to be in his sixties just like I am now. That may seem like a long time away, but it'll get here sooner than you think. When someone asks him to remember something about his childhood, what will he talk about? The lunches he had and hated when he was in day care? The times when Mom was so busy doing something for everyone else that she didn't have time for him? The times she had to stay late at work, so she missed the pizza he

What You Can Do

- Don't expect perfection. Nobody's perfect, and you and your son will both make your share of mistakes.
- Use your words wisely.
- Focus on connection, not activities or stuff.
- Love him unconditionally.

"cooked" especially for her and the brownie recipe he invented, using powdered milk instead of flour?

Or will he talk about autumn afternoons and drinking a cup of hot chocolate while Mom read him his favorite book? Will he laugh about the wagon rides she gave him on the way to the grocery store to pick up a gallon of milk? Will he remember the way she smelled as she hugged him close when he fell off his bicycle and then gently washed his knee and put on a Sesame Street bandage?

Connect with your son, and you'll hold his heart for a lifetime.

By the way, tomato soup is still one of my favorites, made with a dab of butter floating on top just like my mom used to make it. Try it sometime. I bet you'll like it too. It's mmm-mmm, good!

Epilogue

Good Ol' Mom

I'd never be where I am today if it weren't for my mom, who believed in me despite all evidence to the contrary.

I'm a man. I burp. I grunt. I like to be in charge of the television remote. And sometimes all I need to converse with another man? A nod. Yep, that'll do.

But when you get deep down inside Kevin Leman, you'll find I'm also a softie. Especially when it comes to my mom.

Recently I was speaking at a Hearts at Home conference in Rochester, Minnesota. A group called Go Fish entertained the women with songs. The last song was a medley, including a contemporary version of "Jesus Loves Me."

I was supposed to get up and talk for 45 minutes about my book *Have a New Kid by Friday*. The timer flashed with three minutes to go. But as I sat backstage, listening to that song, I got misty-eyed. I started thinking of my dear, sweet mom.

When the timer beeped, I walked out onstage and sat on the stool quietly for a moment. Then I looked at the women in the audience. "You know, I didn't plan on saying what I'm going to say. But that last song got to me. It made me think of my dear, sweet mom, who prayed for me every day. I want you ladies to know something. What you are doing—the sacrifices you're making in your lives as moms every day—is *really worth it*. I stand here today before you only because I had a mom who believed in me despite all good evidence to the contrary."

I went on to tell them about my mother, my growing-up years, and the plaque she hung in my bedroom—a plaque I hated for years until I grew to understand its meaning.

> *I had a mom who believed in me despite all good evidence to the contrary.*

Even though my mom was married to a drinker and a man who wanted nothing to do with church, May Leman was faithful to her Maker. She dragged us kids to church every Sunday. And when I say "dragged us," that's exactly what I mean. We didn't have a car, and my mother didn't know how to drive anyway, so we walked or hitched a ride with someone. But my mother was insistent we kids go to church, even if Dad stayed home.

My mother even signed me up for confirmation, where children learn the basics of the Christian faith . . . and it was on Saturday morning. The one day of the week I had "free" to do as I wish, and I was stuck at church. How I hated that!

Yet just two years ago in Modesto, California, I had the privilege of spending two precious hours with the man who taught that confirmation class. He was also the pastor of that church and was very much a part of my life growing up, thanks to my mom. Those were two of the best hours of my life as we chuckled and laughed, reliving the memories.

Then we talked about that confirmation class. "Cub," he said (my nickname as a kid), "you were the only kid I ever had in that confirmation class who legitimately should have flunked. You just gave things a lick and a holler. I still have a copy of your final exam. I never threw it out because I found it so interesting. When I asked on the final exam, 'What does confirmation mean to you?' I was intending for students to write from their hearts what learning of the Christian faith meant to them. And what did you write?"

He grinned. "You wrote, 'It means that I have to get up early on Saturday morning, get on a stupid bus, and come here.' That was your entire answer.

"And when I asked another time, 'Why did Paul go to Corinth?' your answer was, 'Because he heard the fish were biting there.'"

I embarrassed my mother. Often.

I laughed at that one, because I've always been a fisherman. My buddy Moonhead calls me the "king of the creek" because when we were growing up, I was always fishing in the creek half a mile from my home. And in western New York, you could fish from late spring through early winter. One of the indelible imprints in my mind is fishing when I was 5 years old and looking up at a ledge that was probably 20 feet above the creek. My mom was sitting there on a chair, watching me fish.

You see, for all my antics, my mother wanted to spend time with me, and that time she spent with me made me understand that she loved me no matter what.

Yes, I embarrassed my mother. Often. In fact, I think she attended school more than I did some years (most often in the principal's office), since I'd cut school on Mondays and Fridays with great regularity. My mother would show up for parent-teacher conferences (oh, what she must have suffered, going through each one), and every time she talked to a teacher, she'd get the same litany: "Kevin has the ability if he'd just apply himself." After hearing this over and over for years, my mother had little reason to believe in me, but she believed in me anyway.

Moms, if you're going to err, err on the side of believing in your child. Expect the best out of them, believe the best of them . . . but don't let them get away with squat either. Bailing your kids out of trouble at every turn won't help any of you in the long run.

Keep the focus on your connection, your relationship. Even when I was a screwup for all those years, I could still talk to my mother about anything. We had a close relationship. (Take a look around at how many high schoolers are still confiding in their mothers, and you'll know what an unusual relationship my mother and I had.) I trusted her. And today I'm a good dad because of my mom's input on my life—because of her consistency and example.

But there came a time when I, as my mother's son, had to step up to the plate for myself.

Without my mother, I would never have come to faith—without her dragging me to church and laying the foundation for me, even when it didn't seem like her actions or words were making a difference at all.

But there came a time when I, as my mother's son, had to step up to the plate for myself. That was when I was graduating from high school, and I realized all of a sudden, "Hey, my buddies are going to college. What am I going to do?"

I was going nowhere. I had applied to numerous colleges and universities. No one would have me. The University of Buffalo night school turned me down. The technical community college turned me down. I was finally allowed into our church denomination's school—on probation, no less—just nine days before school started. Dad cashed in a life insurance policy he had to send me there, so through fear and hard work, I managed to pull a C+ average my freshman year. When I didn't have the money to go back the next year, I stayed out a trimester. I went back the next trimester because I wanted to play baseball on the college team—now *that* was motivation to this young man—but got thrown out of school for a college prank gone wrong (stealing money out of the conscience fund).

That's when I ended up in Tucson as a janitor.

Was this the kind of life my mother had dreamed for me, her son, when she first held little Kevin Leman in her arms?

Was this the kind of life my mother had dreamed for me, her son, when she first held little Kevin Leman in her arms? I'm sure it wasn't. Yet sometimes life unfurls in unexpected ways, in bits and pieces.

For me, getting that job as a janitor was just another page in my journey to figuring out that's not how I wanted to spend the rest of my life. And during that time as a janitor, I met Sande, my wife, and came to faith in God.

Never once did my mother treat me as a loser. Never did I feel condemnation from her for who I was. She simply encouraged me and continued to believe that I, Kevin Leman, was someone special and could become whatever I wanted to be.

With that in mind, my mother had bought me a plaque when I was young. (She must have known this boy would need some additional, ever-present encouragement to make something of himself.) She hung it right in the center of the wall in my bedroom. No, I didn't like it. In fact, having that plaque in my room embarrassed me.

When my friends Jamie and Moonhead came over to play, we'd always end up flat-bellied on my bedroom floor, playing with plastic cowboys or arguing over a board game of some kind. And over our heads hung that ever-present plaque, compliments of Mom, all my growing-up years. I knew better than to try to take it down, because she'd put it right back up.

Yet some 50 years later, I can still remember the words of that plaque:

Only one life,
'Twill soon be past.
Only what's done
For Christ will last.

Mom, sometimes you may think that everything you do for your son is for nothing. That it doesn't make a difference. That he isn't really listening to anything you say. That nothing is getting through.

But take it from this son, all grown up (well, mostly!). Your son is watching everything you do and listening to everything you say. You can count on it. It's guaranteed.

So don't sell yourself short. You make a difference. And I'm living proof of it every day.

The Top 10 Countdown
to Being an Awesome Mom

10. Remember, he's a boy, not a girl.
9. I know he's adorable, but he needs to be held accountable.
8. Don't always pay attention to how he looks; pay more attention to his heart.
7. How you handle his failures is more important than how you handle his victories.
6. No two children in a family should be treated the same, because they're not the same—including your boy.
5. Remember that your boy will only stay weird for about 15 years.
4. He's the wavy line—all over the place. You need to be the consistent one.
3. Start with the end in mind. Who do you want your son to be?
2. You don't get to relive moments. Make every day count.
1. Many have tried, and no one's succeeded—you can't do it all. But what you do will make a lasting difference in the life of your son.

Notes

Chapter 1 Your Boy Doesn't Need to Wear a Skirt

1. Paul Candon, "Brain Structure May Influence Male-Female Behavior Differences," *New York Times Syndicate*, December 15, 1999, http://nytsyn.com.

2. Jane Everhart, "Male, Female Differences Can Impact Treatment Regimens," *New York Times Syndicate*, December 15, 1999, http://nytsyn.com.

3. Ibid.

4. Jennifer Cox, ed., "Understanding the Human Brain," *Children's Britannica*, Encyclopedia Britannica, Inc., 136–41, accessed December 7, 2008, http://www.sfu.ca/~dkimura/articles/britan.htm.

5. "Benjamin S. Carson, M.D.," Academy of Achievement, November 11, 2010, http://www.achievement.org/autodoc/page/car1bio-1.

Chapter 2 Planning Your Toddler's Wedding

1. Jem Aswad, "Usher Sounds Off about Marriage, His Mom, and the Challenge of Being a Superstar Dad," June 12, 2008, http://www.mtv.com/news/articles/1589159/20080611/usher.jhtml.

Chapter 3 What Kind of Parent Are You?

1. Ephesians 6:1.

2. Quiz answers

Authoritarian

"I *told* you to do it."

"Are you sure you're done with your homework?"

"I don't care what you think about dinner. Just eat it!"

"Go back to bed now. I put you in bed once; I'm not putting you there again—and no, you can't have a drink of water!"
Permissive
"Oh, don't worry about it. Mommy can do it for you."
"Of course, I'll make sure you have that special shirt for tomorrow."
"I told you that you couldn't have that. . . . Well, all right . . . just this once."
3. Ephesians 6:1.

Chapter 4 Understanding Fletcher

1. Quick Quiz answers:
The Middleborn
He goes out of his way to avoid conflicts. He's the mediator and very diplomatic. He is loyal to his many friends and compromises so that others will like him. He is independent, a maverick, and secretive. He's not used to having attention at home, so he finds it elsewhere—in his peers.
The Firstborn
You can always count on him. He is a natural leader, takes life seriously (including his studies), is a perfectionist, and is well organized. He loves to read. He's conscientious, critical, logical, technically oriented, and a list maker. He drives himself (and others) and doesn't like surprises.
The Baby of the Family
He's a charmer, an attention seeker, and a people person. He could sell ice to Eskimos. He is engaging, is affectionate, and loves surprises. The world revolves around him. He blames others when something goes wrong (it's never his fault). He often gets away with murder because he's cute.
The Only Child
He is a little adult and feels more comfortable with people who are older or younger. He's self-motivated, a voracious reader, and a high achiever. He thinks in black and white—no grays allowed—and talks in extremes ("always," "never"). He's very thorough in everything he does and expects a lot out of himself. He is cautious and can't stand the idea of failing at any task.
2. See Kevin Leman, *The Birth Order Book* (Grand Rapids: Revell), 2009.

Chapter 6 Ages and Stages #1

1. Proverbs 22:6 (NIV).

Chapter 8 Guess What His Favorite Body Part Is

1. Mike Tierney, "With Nine Mouths to Feed, Travis Henry Says He's Broke," *New York Times*, March 11, 2009, http://www.nytimes.com/2009/03/12/sports/football/12henry.html.

Chapter 9 Doormat, Dishrag, or Strong and Smart?

1. For more information, see Alfred Adler, *The Practice and Theory of Individual Psychology* (London: Routledge & Kegan Paul, 1923).

2. Rudolph Dreikurs, *Fundamentals of Adlerian Psychology* (Chicago: Alfred Adler Institute, 1953), 35.

Chapter 10 On Duty or MIA?

1. "Tom Cruise," Yahoo! Movies, accessed December 14, 2009, http://movies.yahoo.com/movie/contributor/1800015725/bio.

Chapter 12 Your Someday Man

1. Robert Putnam and Christine Goss, "It's About Time," *The San Francisco Chronicle*, September 24, 2000, cited in Brian Robertson, "Why Daycare Subsidies Do Not Help Parents or Kids," published by the Family Research Council (Washington DC).

2. "Elvis and His Mother: Gladys Love Presley," ElvisPresleyNews.com, accessed December 13, 2009, http://www.elvispresleynews.com/Elvis-GladysPresley.html.

About Dr. Kevin Leman

An internationally known psychologist, radio and television personality, and speaker, Dr. Kevin Leman has taught and entertained audiences worldwide with his wit and commonsense psychology.

The *New York Times* bestselling and award-winning author of *Have a New Kid by Friday, Have a New Teenager by Friday, Have a New Husband by Friday, Have a New You by Friday, Sheet Music,* and *The Birth Order Book* has made thousands of house calls for radio and television programs, including *Fox & Friends, The View,* Fox's *The Morning Show, Today, Oprah,* CBS's *The Early Show, In the Market with Janet Parshall, Live with Regis Philbin,* CNN's *American Morning,* and *Focus on the Family.* Dr. Leman has also served as a contributing family psychologist to *Good Morning America.*

Dr. Leman is the founder and president of Couples of Promise, an organization designed and committed to help couples remain happily married. His professional affiliations include the American Psychological Association, the

American Federation of Television and Radio Artists, and the North American Society of Adlerian Psychology.

In 2003, the University of Arizona awarded Dr. Leman the highest award they can give to one of their own: the Distinguished Alumnus Award. In 2010, North Park University awarded him an honorary Doctor of Humane Letters degree.

Dr. Leman received his bachelor's degree in psychology from the University of Arizona, where he later earned his master's and doctorate degrees. Originally from Williamsville, New York, he and his wife, Sande, live in Tucson, Arizona. They have five children and two grandchildren.

For information regarding speaking availability, business consultations, seminars, or the annual Couples of Promise cruise, please contact:

Dr. Kevin Leman
P.O. Box 35370
Tucson, Arizona 85740
Phone: (520) 797-3830
Fax: (520) 797-3809
www.birthorderguy.com
www.drleman.com

Resources
by Dr. Kevin Leman

Books for Adults

Have a New Kid by Friday
Have a New Husband by Friday
Have a New You by Friday
Have a New Teenager by Friday
The Birth Order Book
Under the Sheets
Sheet Music
Making Children Mind without Losing Yours
Born to Win
Sex Begins in the Kitchen
It's Your Kid, Not a Gerbil
7 Things He'll Never Tell You . . . But You Need to Know
What Your Childhood Memories Say about You
Running the Rapids
What a Difference a Mom Makes

What a Difference a Daddy Makes
The Way of the Shepherd (written with William Pentak)
The Way of the Wise
Becoming the Parent God Wants You to Be
Becoming a Couple of Promise
A Chicken's Guide to Talking Turkey with Your Kids about Sex (written with Kathy Flores Bell)
First-Time Mom
Step-parenting 101
Living in a Stepfamily without Getting Stepped On
The Perfect Match
Be Your Own Shrink
Stopping Stress before It Stops You
Single Parenting That Works
Why Your Best Is Good Enough
Smart Women Know When to Say No

Books for Children, with Kevin Leman II

My Firstborn, There's No One Like You
My Middle Child, There's No One Like You
My Youngest, There's No One Like You
My Only Child, There's No One Like You
My Adopted Child, There's No One Like You
My Grandchild, There's No One Like You

DVD/Video Series for Group Use

Have a New Kid by Friday
Making Children Mind without Losing Yours (Christian—parenting edition)

Making Children Mind without Losing Yours (Mainstream—public school teacher edition)
Value-Packed Parenting
Making the Most of Marriage
Running the Rapids
Single Parenting That Works
Bringing Peace and Harmony to the Blended Family

DVDs for Home Use

Straight Talk on Parenting
Why You Are the Way You Are
Have a New Husband by Friday
Have a New You by Friday

Available at 1-800-770-3830, www.birthorderguy.com, or www.drleman.com

Take the
5-Day Challenge

Family expert Dr. Kevin Leman reveals in this *New York Times* bestseller why your kids do what they do, and what you can do about it—in just five days!

Kid-tested,
parent-approved

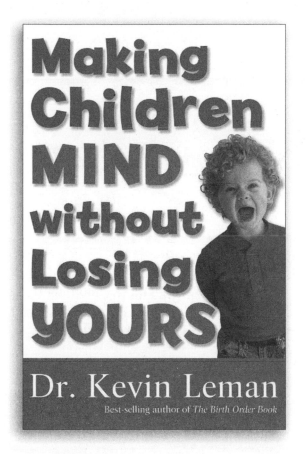

If anyone understands why children behave the way they do, it's Dr. Kevin Leman. In this bestseller he equips parents with seven principles of reality discipline—a loving, no-nonsense parenting approach that really works.

My child used to be normal.
What happened?

"Congratulations! You have a teenager in your home. Life will never quite be the same again. . . . But it can be better than you've ever dreamed. I guarantee it."—Dr. Kevin Leman

Have a new husband by Friday?

Is that even possible?

Dr. Kevin Leman says it is. The *New York Times* bestselling author and relationship expert shows you how with his easy and accessible principles.

Make your marriage *sizzle!*

Learn to build communication, affection, consideration, and caring in your marriage to make it more emotionally— and physically—satisfying.

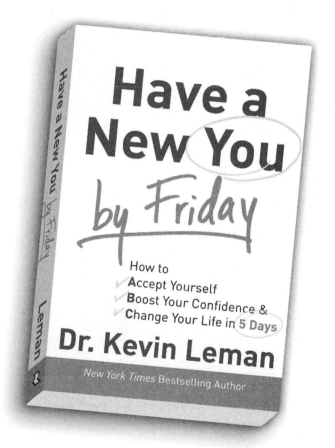

You Can Reduce Stress and Enjoy Your Life

Bestselling author Dr. Kevin Leman helps you manage the six stress points in your life: kids, career, husband, housework, money, and crammed schedules.

Learn How to Set
Healthy Boundaries

This bestselling author uses commonsense psychology,
humor, and stories to help women learn how to live
a more balanced life.

ℛ Revell

a division of Baker Publishing Group
www.RevellBooks.com

Available wherever books are sold.

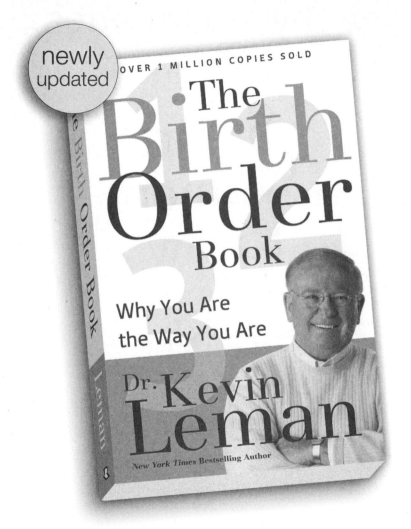